Learn to Paint

ANIMALS

Jean Parry-Williams

COLLINS

First published in 1983
by William Collins Sons & Co., Ltd
London · Glasgow · Sydney
Auckland · Toronto · Johannesburg

Reprinted 1985
New edition 1986

Designed and edited by Youé and Spooner Limited
Filmset by Butler & Tanner Limited

ISBN 0 00 412117 1

Printed and bound in Spain
by Graficas Reunidas S.A., Madrid

CONTENTS

PORTRAIT OF AN ARTIST
JEAN PARRY-WILLIAMS

Jean Parry-Williams was brought up in the country and lived in a home which was always full of animals. Her house was situated on the Cheshire-Derbyshire borders and so she was well placed to visit all the fine galleries and museums in and around Manchester. This, coupled with the encouragement of her father who took her from an early age to see paintings whenever possible, has made her one of the lucky ones. She says of herself, 'although perhaps not born with a silver spoon in my mouth, I was certainly blessed with a pencil in my hand.'

In the 1930s Jean Parry-Williams won several children's drawing competitions, run by the *Manchester Guardian*, with scenes of animals set in local surround-

ings. During her school days she took Honours in all the Royal Drawing Society examinations and won a special prize for drawing animals. Also during this time she exhibited in the National Children's Academy in London run by the *Sunday Mirror*. After leaving school she studied at the Royal Salford College of Art and then spent a year in Vienna at a well-known studio and was thrilled to have the chance of studying from the portfolios of original drawings by Albrecht Dürer. Here, too, she was lucky enough to attend and sketch the rehearsals of the famous Lipizzaner horses in the Spanish Riding School.

Jean has exhibited in various provincial and London

The steeplechaser *High Clouds* 41 × 51cm (16 × 20in)

open exhibitions, including the Royal Academy, and has had her own shows of mixed-media paintings held in London. These shows also toured the provinces. However, animal portraiture began to take up more and more of her time as commissions started to come her way. When she lived in Hampshire, the local paper, the *Southern Evening Echo*, commissioned her to write and illustrate several articles after seeing some of her work done during an annual sketching visit to Crufts Dog Show. Later, on moving to Gloucestershire, *Cotswold Life* magazine also published several articles with animals as the central theme. Jean writes and illustrates articles for the *Leisure Painter* and regularly

gives lectures and demonstrations for Daler-Rowney. In addition, she works as a freelance lecturer for various Colleges of Further Education and is the tutor for the Pitman Pastel Correspondence Course. She also runs small painting classes from her own studio in Painswick, Gloucestershire.

Although Jean Parry-Williams specializes in animal portraiture and has appeared on television demonstrating this, her favourite subject, she also enjoys painting landscapes, seascapes, still life and portraits in oil, watercolour and pastel. Her paintings are in many private collections throughout the United Kingdom and as far afield as Denmark, Pakistan and the USA.

WHY PAINT ANIMALS?

There are many reasons! You may want to have a record of a favourite dog or cat and a quick sketch or finished drawing would be just the thing. Or perhaps you want to be more ambitious and paint an oil, watercolour or pastel portrait to hang on your wall as a reminder of a beloved pet who is no longer with you. Or you may just love animals and want to portray some of their beauty and character in a drawing or painting. Photographs seem to lack some of the vitality of a drawing or painting and although animal portraiture poses many problems, you may feel you want to take up the challenge and try to capture on paper or canvas some of the personality, mood, expression and even humour of an animal. I hope I can help you do this.

How often, when painting a landscape, have you felt that animals placed here and there would just complete the picture? Perhaps your scene is a Welsh or Scottish hillside, with sheep in the distance. Maybe you are painting a view of meadows with cattle steadily munching among the grasses, or lying contentedly chewing the cud. Sometimes, a group of horses make a colourful picture grazing in their paddock or standing alert watching some distant object. In each case, if you are not sure of their basic shapes you will probably leave them out, wishing all the time that you were more confident and able to paint them.

Animals have a natural grace and rhythm which you may long to capture in a picture. Even when still they have a pent-up force which can be released in a moment; this is the essence of most animals. Even a sleeping dog or cat is always on guard. There is the speed of a galloping horse

with its flowing mane and tail; the ripple of underlying muscles and the bone structure of a fleet-footed greyhound; and even cows, calves and pigs can have sudden surges of movement.

These to me are all very good reasons for wanting to learn to paint animals and I hope I can help you gain the confidence to do just that.

Keeping a Scrapbook

I find it very useful to keep a scrapbook of newspaper and magazine cuttings of animals. It provides an invaluable source of reference material if there is no model immediately available and you want to check a position or a point of anatomy. It can also spark off ideas and give you inspiration when you have one of those blank periods. Be methodical with your collection and keep different animals together, i.e. dogs in one place, cats in another. I don't stick down my cuttings but keep them loose in their sections so that I can easily take them out for reference. This also facilitates increasing or discarding parts of the collection. Specialist animal books which often have anatomical details can be helpful but you can't beat the real thing. Work from nature as much as you can, in every possible situation.

Choosing a Subject

When you set out to draw or paint an animal you must choose your subject carefully, especially if you are a beginner. Unlike human models you cannot rely on your animal model staying in the same position for very long (unless, of course, it is asleep). I always try and train my own dogs to sit still for long periods. In fact, a dog to me is more than a special member of the household, it is my assistant and model at many painting demonstrations. Ideally, one's subject should have good proportions and features, well-defined muscle and bone structure and an intelligent, attractive face. It is also much easier to draw and paint an animal who has a kind and docile nature. But if you are painting someone else's animal you will obviously have to get used to the animal possibly being nervous, irritable and moving around a lot. On such an occasion it is useful to make quick outline sketches, not only to familiarize yourself with the animal, but so that you have several different positions to choose from.

On the opposite page you can study three paintings of my puppy, Tess. A lot of careful thought and many sketches of different poses preceded these (see also pages 44-45). I cannot stress enough the need to make preliminary sketches and to draw, many times, every animal you want to paint.

Jean Pardy Williams.
1979.

USING A SKETCHBOOK

LIKE ALL ANIMALS, DUCKS KEEP ON THE MOVE SO KEEP THE LINES FLOWING. THESE ARE WHITE AYLESBURYS.

BROKEN EDGES TO OUTLINES GIVES FLUFFY EFFECT

TAWNY OWL

I HAVE SIMPLIFIED THE PLUMAGE INTO ESSENTIAL SHAPES AND MARKINGS.

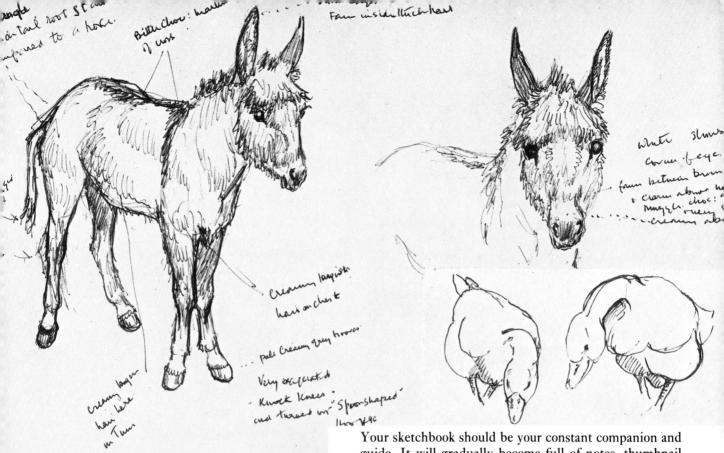

(sketchbook annotations, partially legible:)

a tail root so that...

...pared to a horse.

Bitter Choc... markings... 9 cons

Farm inside... heart

white shows corner of eye

form between brow & crown about... muzzle choc... mealy... cream about...

Creamy largish hair on chest

pale creamy grey trousers

Very complicated Knock Knees and turned in "spoon shaped" those legs

creamy longer hair here in Tum

NOTICE HOW CLOSE EARS ARE TOGETHER, AND HOW LARGE WITH HEAD AND BODY SIZE

Your sketchbook should be your constant companion and guide. It will gradually become full of notes, thumbnail sketches, plans and even finished drawings. Try and carry a small one with you wherever you go and practise drawing at every opportunity – while waiting for the bus, sitting in the park or shopping at the market. Draw anything and everything as it is only by constant practice and observation that you will perfect your drawing. You can sketch while watching television even though a single picture is seldom held for more than a few seconds. Naturally, you should take a sketchbook to any events where there are likely to be animals, for example, the racecourse, local dog shows and country fairs. Make studies of animals at the zoo or at the circus – these places are a great source of information and inspiration.

A sketchbook is a very personal thing because it records an artist's thoughts and ideas as they are forming. It is invaluable to supplement sketches done as preludes to painting with written notes, as you will see from the pages of my sketchbook reproduced here. These notes can be general comments about the animal, its character and personality, or swatches of colour to help you remember the colours accurately when you are back in the studio.

Let me explain here what I mean by a sketch and a drawing. To me, a sketch is a quick, rough impression of a subject caught in a few lines, either in black and white or in colour, whereas a drawing is a detailed study of a subject using all kinds of different mediums. This detailed study can be the preliminary stage before you start the final painting, or it can be a finished drawing in its own right that you may well want to frame and hang on the wall. I always do several careful drawings (as well as preliminary sketches) of an animal before I actually paint it and you will see some of these drawings and sketches on the next few pages.

DRAWING AND SKETCHING MATERIALS

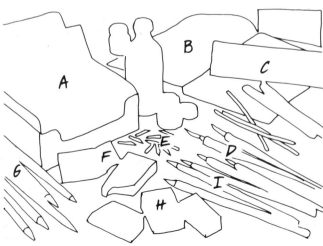

A DRAWING INKS
B SKETCH-PAD
C WILLOW CHARCOAL
D DRAWING PENS
E PEN POINTS
F KNEADABLE PUTTY RUBBER
G BALLPOINT, FELT-TIP PENS
H ERASERS
I PENCILS

I use a great variety of tools to gain the effects that I want when sketching and drawing and you can see some of these in the picture opposite. Throughout the text these and the uses to which I put them are described in some detail but here I am concerned with a general list. Hard and soft degrees of pencils from HB to 6B (the latter is the softest grade) are obvious choices but I also use ballpoint and felt-tip pens, sticks of charcoal and charcoal pencils, Conté crayons and pastels. Conté crayons come in white, black, sanguine (copper coloured) and grey. Throughout this book the pastels I refer to are Artists' Quality Soft Pastels. Students' Quality Pastels are invariably much harder. Fountain pens, Rotring pens, old-fashioned dip pens and indian ink (with a bottle of water so that you can dilute its strength), a kneadable putty rubber and fixative are also essential for most people. Above all do not forget a sketch-pad. I generally use an A3 landscape sketch-pad of white cartridge paper 297 × 420mm ($11\frac{3}{4} \times 16\frac{1}{2}$in).

The drawings of the Jack Russell Terrier were done in ballpoint pen, heightened with Conté crayon and coloured pencils. While doing these drawings I sat on a sofa in his owner's flat drinking coffee, with a biscuit meant for me given in small bits to the little dog to keep his interest. It is often necessary to have little titbits handy. As he moved from one position to another I sketched each one. He had a way of sitting up begging for minutes at a time, crossing one paw over the other and comfortably leaning back on his stumpy tail with his back to the fire. Once he almost dropped off to sleep sitting there bolt upright! Of course you must never laugh at animals. Their feelings are very

easily hurt and once their confidence in you is lost it is very difficult to regain it. Dogs usually keep still better than cats but this cat in my pencil drawing was very helpful. While I was working on sketches for a painting of two dogs, he stalked into the room and watched the proceedings from a suitable vantage point on the back of an armchair. I suddenly became aware of his intense stare. The opportunity was too good to miss, so using a 3B pencil I started to draw him. I quickly sketched in the general body shape and then blocked in the dark areas with cross-hatched lines. Next, I drew the shape of his head, ears, and his eyes. I then worked on the other details and finished by paying attention to his hair markings.

This poodle, however, was a very different type of subject. He had an intense black coat and a cheeky temperament! For my first sketch I used a black medium-tip ballpoint pen. He was finally painted in pastel with the mid-tones of his tight curls in Cool Grey Tint 4 and the highlights on them executed with touches of white Conté, while Burnt Umber Tint 4 was ideal for his dark brown eyes.

Jean Parry-Williams.

very Um 357

Longer hair n...
Longer Curls
on m...

Slightly...
to nose
Nose f...
a little...

Mute
Gold
centre to col...
Silver, gold...
hanging from...

Bell —

Silver

Gold

Blue —

Pale yellow

During one of my animal painting courses, the horse shown here dozed in the warm afternoon sunshine. As my students drew and painted him from various angles, I did a quick sketch of his head. I used a stick of willow charcoal to outline the head shape. For the colours of his neck and head I used the pastels Yellow Ochre Tint 4 with Autumn Brown Tint 3 for the lighter, and Burnt Umber Tint 4 for the darker, tones on his mane. The pink round the muzzle was lightly indicated with Burnt Umber Tint 2 with a touch of Rose Madder Tint 0.

SHAPE AND PROPORTION

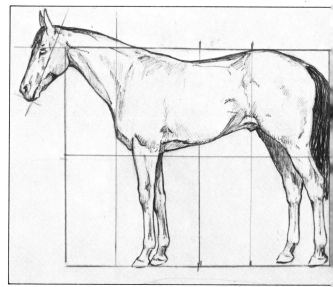

Fig. 1

It is natural for you to want to start work on your final painting as quickly as possible, but you should not rush ahead so fast that you make avoidable mistakes in the drawing stage which are then difficult to put right once you start painting. Once again, I must stress the importance of sketching and drawing. With practice and continuous observation of animals you will become more proficient and will soon be able to avoid the more obvious mistakes in shape, proportion and anatomy. However, until you reach that stage of proficiency, there are a few simple devices which you can include in your preliminary sketches to help you to observe accurately.

All artists have their own method of working. Some base their drawings on stick figures, some on egg shapes or blocks. For my own use I have devised a combination of ideas which may help you to work out the proportions which are so important when drawing animals. Ideally, you should study the anatomy: the skeleton, the shapes of the joints and the limit of their movement, and then look at the underlying muscles. Next, look closely at the animal and see how the skin lies over the muscles and the way the hair grows.

Basic Framework

When you begin to draw an animal a basic framework is helpful. You will find it best to draw an outline of the animal on this framework before you proceed to the smaller details. With experience you will be aware of the relationship between the larger shapes and be able to see the proportions clearly. We will take as an example a 'standard' horse but you can apply these principles to any other animal. Remember that although I say a 'standard' horse, all animals are individuals and vary considerably.

Fig. 1 shows the side view of the standard horse fitted into a basic framework. The horizontal and perpendicular lines help you to sort out the proportion.

Compare the size and proportions of the heavy Suffolk Punch (fig. 2) with the standard horse.

Fig. 3 shows how the front view of a horse's head fits into a 'coffin' shape and how it is equally divided by a perpendicular, central line. The two angles on either side of the top of the 'coffin' show where the ears fit and where the eyes are placed – approximately a quarter of the way down the face on the outer edges of the head. It is useful to choose the head, a prominent feature, as a yardstick against which you can measure other parts of the body.

Fig. 2

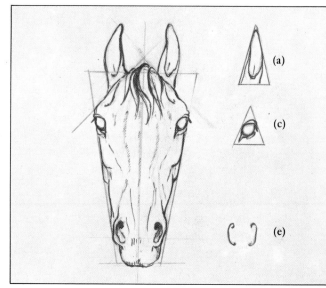

Fig. 3

(b)

(d)

(f)

4

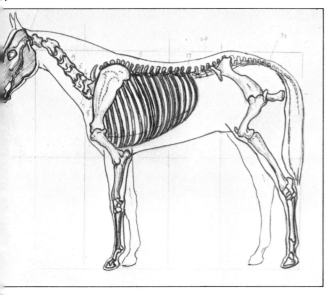

5

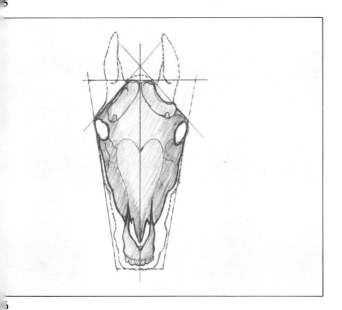

6

If you slant the 'coffin' shape (**fig. 4**) and draw the head within it you will notice how much of the face comes above the central line and how the approximate positions of the various features compare one with another.

In **fig. 5** we can see how the skeleton fits within the outline of the horse. If you study this it is obvious that certain areas of the body are shaped by the underlying bone structure.

In **fig. 6** we see the head again full on. The bones of the skull and its moulding make it clear how the structure of the head is made up.

There are certain 'shorthand' shapes within which parts of the horse's body can be drawn. Look at the full face and side view of the head and you will see how the ears fit into a tall narrow triangle (**a** and **b**). The eye in each case will roughly fit into a triangle (**c** and **d**). Note the eyelashes grow out at an angle, not straight out sideways. Full face, the nostrils are like two commas facing in towards each other (**e** and **f**). From the side, the hooves are a triangle (**g**) but viewed from the front they are a curved wedge-shape (**h**). Depending on how far the ear is swivelled forward, you may or may not see inside it (see **figs. 1** and **4**).

You will find that once you have got the respective sizes and angles right and in proportion, the other details of the animal's anatomy will follow more easily.

Another useful tip is to place an old cardboard mount of a suitable size over the picture you are working on (**fig. 7**). This makes a temporary frame through which to work and helps you to bring the whole image into the right scale and proportion. Alternatively, you can use two right-angled pieces of card which can be overlapped to form the correct image area and to show the effect of a coloured mount surrounding the painting.

Fig. 7

ANATOMY AND FORESHORTENING

Anatomy

When you have had some practice in drawing a particular animal, you will begin to get a feel for its anatomy and will be able to judge whether a particular pose is possible or not. Do not forget to consult your animal anatomy books and remember that photographs can help enormously at this stage. Obviously, there is not the space to go into detail here about anatomy and indeed it is a complicated subject which would fill a whole book, but often it can help to run your hands through the fur of an animal to feel the structure beneath – for example, how the legs bend. This is especially helpful when the length of an animal's fur tends to obscure the details of its anatomy. You can see this in my portrait of the little white dog in oils on pages 39-41.

Beware of one common anatomical mistake: the legs of an animal – so often the beginner gets their anatomy wrong. The joint at roughly the mid-point of the hind legs is the ankle and not, as one might expect, the knee. Consequently, it does not bend in the way a knee would; it bends backwards. Of course, with the front legs, the knees bend in the same way as human knees.

In my colour sketch of the resting greyhound, you can see the muscle and bone formation – the leg tendons are especially noticeable. I often find it helpful to compare my own bone structure with that of the animal I'm drawing. The animal kingdom has the same skeleton and skull formation as humans, but various areas differ in proportion e.g. the neck of a giraffe is very much longer than that of a human! Also, some joints are positioned differently e.g. the knee and elbow joints in a horse and a human being.

Foreshortening

Foreshortening takes place when a shape is turned at such an angle to you that what you see appears elongated or shortened, or you see something exaggerated as in the 'front-on' views of the St Bernard and the horse illustrated on page 17.

If you look at **figs. 8** and **9**, you will see that viewed from the front, the body of the horse is compressed into the shape of an upright barrel – or should I say, several barrels, receding away from you. It is always useful to draw two vertical guidelines when doing this kind of foreshortened view of an animal, as you will find it easier to work within such a framework. The shoulders and chest of the horse are then compressed into a second barrel-shape and then back on the furthest plane you see the curve of the belly and top of the hindquarters.

In my sketches of the greyhound, which are good examples of foreshortening, the distance from nose-tip to shoulder appears greater than from the shoulder to the tail. This is a considerable exaggeration since in a straightforward profile the shoulder-tail distance would be the greater.

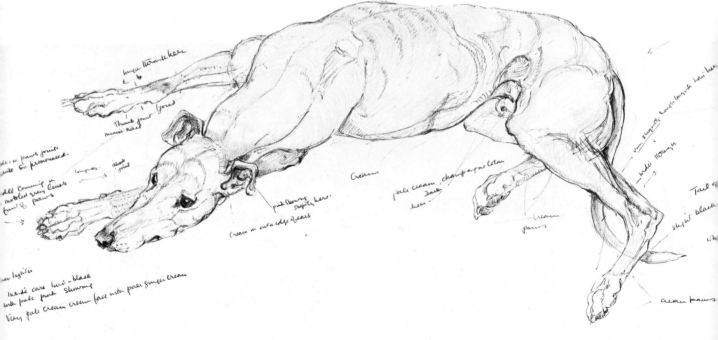

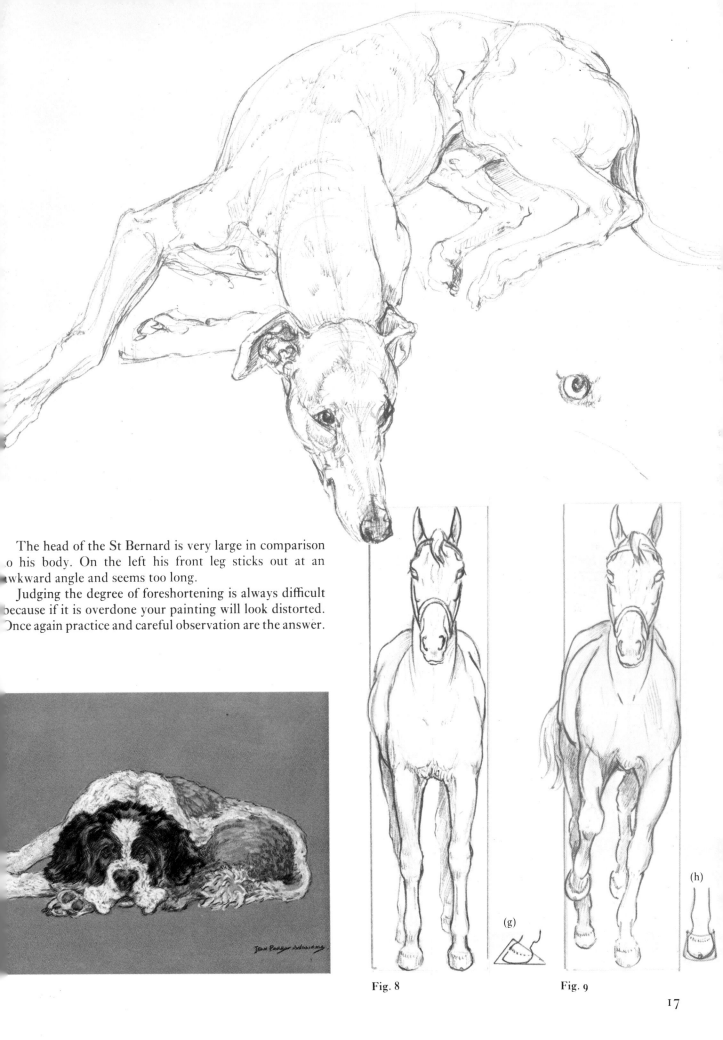

The head of the St Bernard is very large in comparison to his body. On the left his front leg sticks out at an awkward angle and seems too long.

Judging the degree of foreshortening is always difficult because if it is overdone your painting will look distorted. Once again practice and careful observation are the answer.

(g)

(h)

Fig. 8

Fig. 9

USING PASTELS AND CHARCOAL

Pastels

Pastel drawing can be said to have originated in prehistoric times when early cavemen drew animals and hunters on cave walls, using coloured earths. Some of these fascinating paintings, often up to two metres high, can be seen in the caves of France and Spain, the most famous being at Lascaux in S.W. France. Modern pastels are made by adding to the pigment an inert substance such as china clay to control their strength. Artists' Quality Soft Pastels range in tint strength from 0, when a large quantity of clay is added, to 8, which contains a large amount of pigment, and hence is a much stronger colour. Soft pastels are one of the most stable mediums that an artist can use and are highly regarded by professionals. Artists' Quality pastels are called 'soft' because this describes their character (a few are hard in certain colours at their greatest strength). There are varieties of cheap pastels which are hard and difficult to use because they are scratchy and so I do not recommend them. Artists' Quality Soft Pastels have their tint number on the wrapper together with their name. An extensive range of colours and tint strengths are available.

I break my pastel sticks into short lengths, using the sharp broken edge for line work and the side for thick sweeps of colour where I need to fill a large area with solid colour. Personally, I find pastel one of the best mediums for painting animals as it is especially good for portraying hair and fur such as the dense quality of a heavy-coated large dog like an Old English Sheepdog; the soft fur of a cat or the smooth satin-like texture of the glossy coat of a well-groomed horse. A great variety of colours are obtainable and these can be mixed either by placing tints in short strokes side by side, or by painting dots of different colour very close together, as did some of the French Impressionist painters like Seurat. One pastel can also be lightly imposed over another to make yet another colour. You can blend the colours together by rubbing them in with a stump of finely rolled paper, or your fingers. You can fix the pastel and work on top of it; in short you can use it in a great variety of ways.

Oil Pastels

Oil pastels are made by mixing the pigment with an oil and wax. They were invented by a Frenchman in the nineteenth century but have only become available comparatively recently for general use. The best are available in a large number of tints. They are compatible with oil paints and can be blended with turpentine to produce a wash effect. They should not be used in conjunction with Artists' Quality Soft Pastels. They are particularly useful for quick sketching on the spot.

Paper

As with the pastels themselves, there are a large variety of papers to choose from. They come in different weights, colours and textures, but it is advisable to have a paper which is tough enough to stand erasing and with enough roughness or 'tooth' to hold amounts of pastel loaded on to it. If the paper is too thin it will show tiny creases and may tear when you are rubbing out. Colours vary and you will obviously choose those which will give a suitable background for the type of picture you are painting. For most animal work I generally use a pale fawny-beige pastel paper, but with black or white animals a stone coloured or grey-toned pastel paper is better. Some artists use a white watercolour paper which they tint with a suitable colour wash.

Charcoal

Charcoal is made from the thin peeled twigs of the lime or willow which are heated to glowing point, without the free access of air, until they are completely carbonized. Lime and willow woods are best as they are free of resin and give a rich colour. Any wood containing resin, such as fir or pine, produces a vegetable tar which, when carbonized, would smear if used for drawing.

Boxes of charcoal sticks can be purchased from most art supply stockists. These sticks are rather fragile to handle, but pleasing in richness and depth of tone. They can be broken and used in short lengths. It is not necessary to sharpen them as the broken end can be used to give a sharply defined line. The sides of the broken short lengths can also be used to add shadow and texture. The sticks come in various thicknesses, from thin to thick, the thickest are called 'scene painters charcoal' in England.

Charcoal is also made into pencils. The charcoal is compressed and inserted into wooden sheaths in the same way that a lead pencil is made. The charcoal pencil does not break as easily as the stick of charcoal and it can be sharpened to a point. Such charcoal pencils are available in various strengths from hard to soft in a similar way to an ordinary lead pencil. Charcoal may be used on any paper suitable for pastel painting.

If you wish to lift out a single mistake a kneadable putty

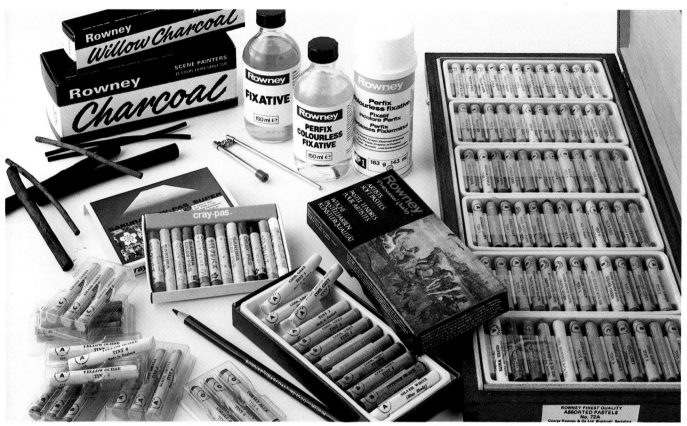

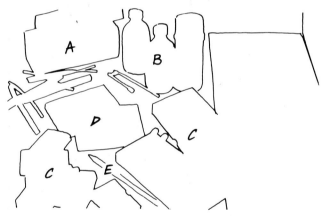

A CHARCOAL
B FIXATIVES & SPRAY DIFFUSER
C ARTISTS' QUALITY SOFT PASTELS
D OIL PASTELS
E CHARCOAL PENCIL

rubber is best. If a large area is wrong, use a clean cotton rag – smack the paper with the rag or rub it over the surface. One tip which may be useful if you should have to erase and find you have mislaid your putty rubber – the soft inside of new bread works wonders! But do be careful not to include the butter if you are eating sandwiches out of doors. I have still not discovered how to get rid of grease marks on paper!

Fixative

If you wish to protect your pastel and charcoal work against smudging, you should consider preserving it under glass or using a fixative – or both. Charcoal spray fixatives contain a shellac to coat the drawing and stop the particles of charcoal moving or becoming smudged. For pastels, a PVA-based resin in aerosol form is preferable. However, all fixatives do, very slightly, dull the colours. When using an aerosol fixative always spray in a well-ventilated space, preferably out of doors.

Although I use more pastels than those mentioned in this book, I suggest that beginners start with a basic palette of the colours listed below:

Ivory Black	White (Cream Shade)
Cool Grey Tint 4	Cobalt Blue Tint 6
Prussian Blue Tint 1	Yellow Ochre Tint 4
Sap Green Tint 5, 8	Lizard Green Tint 3
Autumn Brown Tint 3	Burnt Sienna Tint 2
Burnt Umber Tint 6	
Black charcoal pencils	Black charcoal sticks,
Conté crayons: black,	thick and thin
grey, white, sanguine	

USING OILS

Oil painting became popular in the sixteenth and seventeenth centuries, although pigments had first been mixed with an oil binder several centuries earlier. Today sunflower, poppy and linseed oils are the main binding agents mixed with pigments.

Artists' Quality Oil Colours are the best available. Beginners, for whom price might be a consideration, should use Rowney Georgian Oil Colours.

With oils, colours do not run into each other as they can with watercolours. So, different colours can be applied next to each other or on top of each other and they will not mix unless worked in with a brush. As the paint remains malleable for several hours, it is encouraging for the beginner to know that any mistakes can be wiped away with a rag, or painted over.

Basic Equipment for the Beginner

1. A set of good quality oil paints (see page 21). Some suggested colours for your basic palette: Titanium White, Ivory Black, Cobalt Blue, Viridian, Lemon Yellow, Naples Yellow, Yellow Ochre, Cadmium Yellow Deep, Burnt Umber, Burnt Sienna, Crimson Alizarin (or Indian Red). I always use Crimson Alizarin but it is a very strong colour and should be used sparingly. If you find it too strong you could use Indian Red instead. With these colours you can mix all the colours needed for most pictures. There is, however, an enormous range of oil paints from which to choose if you do wish to expand your palette later.
2. A box to hold your paints.
3. A palette on which to arrange and mix your paints (see page 21).
4. A palette knife for mixing your colours and to scrape off unwanted paint.
5. One bottle of pure turpentine and one of linseed oil.
6. A double dipper (or two single ones). One dipper holds your thinning medium which can be either turpentine or turpentine mixed with linseed oil, depending on the stage you have reached in your painting. The other dipper is to hold turpentine for cleaning your brushes whilst painting.
7. A sturdy, folding easel which will take reasonably large as well as small canvases and can be used either indoors or outdoors.
8. A lightweight stool if you want to sit down while working.
9. Paint rags or kitchen roll on which to wipe brushes.
10. A selection of brushes. Brushes come in many shapes and sizes and traditionally the most popular are sable hair and hog bristle brushes. There are also brushes made of man-made fibres, such as nylon, available (see below).
11. Stretched canvas or canvas boards on which to paint (see below).

Always buy the best equipment you can afford. If you look after it, it will last for years. This particularly applies to brushes.

When buying canvas or canvas board, it is important to decide upon the texture of canvas surface you want to paint on as it will have a great bearing on the work you produce. For delicate and detailed work, choose a medium or smooth-grained canvas, but if you want a feeling of vigour and strength a rough surface will help give this effect. As prepared canvas on stretchers is very expensive, you can buy canvas on rolls and cut it to the required size, and then put it on stretchers yourself. For everyday work I use canvas boards 51 × 41cm (20 × 16in).

The following brushes would make a good basic stock: Flat Hog Bristle Series 120 No. 4 for early drawing in on canvas, Series 125 No. 12 to fill in backgrounds and Series 123 No. 6 for other work. I also use Nylon brushes Series 220 Nos. 2, 4, 5, 6, 8 and 10. If this series is unavailable Series 233 will do. I find a Sable brush Series 133 No. 4 ideal for painting small details such as eyes, whiskers, etc. It is also useful to have several large No. 6 brushes either Hog Bristle Series 123 or Nylon Series 220 so that you can use a different brush for each colour mix.

Brushes should be rinsed in turpentine or white spirit after use and then washed with soap and water until completely clean. Finally, they should be drawn back into shape between fingers and thumb and left to dry, standing upright in a jar.

Palettes are made in various shapes and sizes. The most common shapes are oval or rectangular. They can be made of wood, plastic, metal or greaseproof paper. I prefer wood. When you have finished painting for the day, scrape off any surplus paint with your knife. Some paint may be hardly used so put it in an airtight container for future use. Then wipe the surface of the palette with a rag dampened with turpentine. It is always best to start with a clean palette, so that when you next want to mix colours they will be clear without old colours showing through.

I always use a palette knife for mixing my paints because if you use your brush the various colours will build up in the ferrule (where the bristles are attached to the base of the handle) and may transfer unwanted colour on to your painting.

Before you start to paint, it is sometimes advisable to tone down the colour of the white canvas as it can be very dazzling, especially out of doors. You can do this by moistening a rag with turpentine which has been mixed with a little dark colour, such as Burnt Umber, and rubbing this

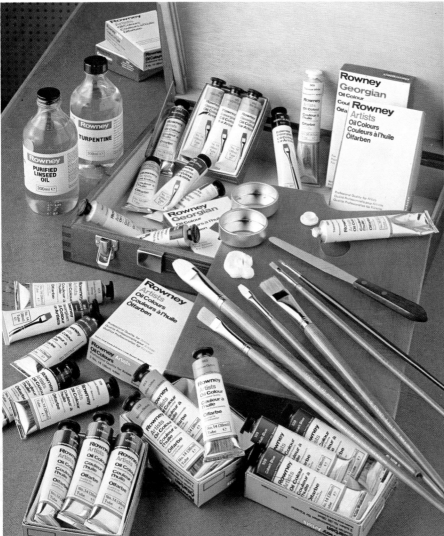

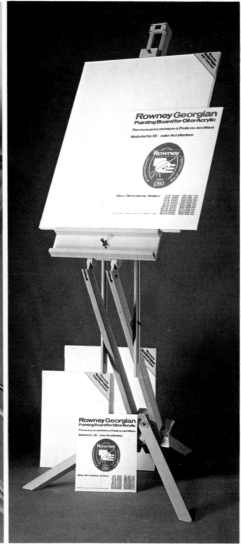

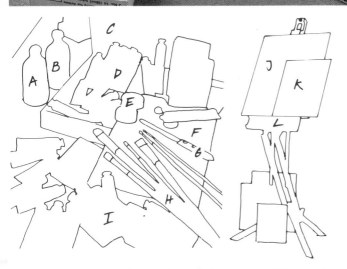

A LINSEED OIL
B TURPENTINE
C PAINT BOX
D GEORGIAN
   OIL COLOURS
E DIPPERS
F PALETTE
G PALETTE KNIFE
H BRUSHES
I ARTISTS'
   OIL COLOURS
J STRETCHED
   CANVAS
K PAINTING BOARD
L EASEL

mixture evenly over the surface of the canvas. When this is dry I make the initial sketch of the subject using a No. 4 brush and Burnt Umber thinned with turpentine. Then I take a rag dipped in this mixture and block in the large shapes and darkest darks. I am then ready to start the actual painting.

Paint can be applied thickly (*impasto*) or thinly, depending on the effect you want. The most usual method is to start with thinly applied colour and build up as the picture progresses, commonly known as 'lean to fat'. This is technically the best way to work but remember that light colours are improved by painting thickly, dark colours are not. Don't be afraid to load your brush with colour and paint it on to the canvas with firm strokes. Some of the pleasures of using oils are the rich texture, the depth of tone you can achieve and the quality of brush strokes.

USING WATERCOLOURS

Watercolour is finely-ground pigment, bound with gum arabic that is soluble in water. It is available in solid or cake form, as well as in tubes. The tubes of Artists' Quality Watercolours have glycerine added to keep them moist. Students' Quality Watercolours are also available.

Watercolour is transparent and when placed on white paper, the paper will show through. This imparts a brightness to the colours that cannot be obtained in other mediums, except perhaps coloured inks. The inexperienced tend to think that watercolour is an easy medium to use, perhaps because they were taught to paint at school with poster colour. Certainly watercolour is convenient to use as you can easily carry around a small box of watercolours with a sketchbook, pencils, some brushes and a small flask of water. However, you need a lot of practice and experience to master watercolour painting and although it is an exciting and exhilarating medium, it can also be very difficult and frustrating!

Whatever subject you choose to paint in watercolour you must give it a lot of thought and planning before you actually start to paint. Sort out your ideas in advance and do several preliminary pencil sketches. Work out where the darks and lights in your picture will fall. Then decide on the correct colour and try to make do with one wash rather than two or more. When you mix up your washes on your palette take care to think of the hue, tone and relative temperature of each colour, red is a hot colour, blue is cold. Spontaneity is part of the charm of watercolour so don't overwork your painting. Also, leave the background impressionistic. Work in broad washes and don't try to put in too much detail – but do treat the main subject with more emphasis than the rest of the painting.

Paints

Your paintbox should have a palette attached to it, usually this forms the lid of the box. The best are made of tin with a white enamelled surface; moulded plastic boxes are also available but these tend to discolour quite easily. Cheaper boxes have paints already in them but with the better ones it is possible to choose your own paints. The colours are in tubes, whole pans and half pans and you will need Artists' Moist Watercolours. When you are starting out I suggest you just buy the following colours: Cadmium Yellow, Burnt Umber, Ivory Black, Cobalt Blue and Crimson Alizarin and add to your palette as you progress.

Brushes

A good selection of brushes to start with would be: Round Sable Series 34 Nos. 6 and 8. If these sable brushes are well cared for they will last a lifetime, but as sables are expensive I can recommend instead Round White Nylon Series 270 Nos. 4, 8, and 12 and Round Mixed Hair Series 60 Nos. 4, 8 and 12.

I manage with only three brushes. One sable: I prefer a No. 6 size (or its equivalent in the excellent nylon brushes) a larger brush of squirrel, badger, or a mixture of hairs (or again nylon) for washes, and a smaller No. 2 or 3 nylon brush for finer details. When choosing a sable brush, test first to see if the bristles will form a point when damp. Ask if you may dip it into clean water, then wipe it and flick off the excess water. If it is a good brush the tip will come to a fine point.

Easels

An easel is useful, especially if you wish to stand when working, and there are a variety to choose from. Buy a sturdy folding one which will double for working outside as well as inside.

Watercolour Paper

This comes in sketchbooks, block pads, or in various sizes of loose sheets. If you use loose sheets of paper, they will have to be mounted on a drawing board either with drawing pins, clips or gummed tape. Watercolour papers come in three surfaces: Rough, Not and Hot Pressed. For the beginner, Not, which has less roughness or 'tooth' is the easiest paper to use as it is neither too thin nor too thick in texture. Paper is also sold by weight. Choose about 300gm² (120-140lb) weight of paper for loose sheets as this heavy paper is firmer and will not cockle so easily.

Stretching Paper

The best way to prevent cockling is to stretch your paper. Take your sheet of paper and completely immerse it in clean water. I use the bath, as you don't want to bend a sheet by pushing it around in a small area such as a basin or sink. When thoroughly wet, hold up the paper by the corner to drain off the excess water. Now place the sheet flat on a wooden drawing board which is slightly larger than the sheet. From a roll of gummed paper-tape cut four lengths which will overlap both the paper and the board. I use a small damp sponge to thoroughly moisten each length of gummed strip which I then place along the edge of each side of the paper in turn, overlapping on to the board. Press down gently but firmly and leave flat overnight to dry naturally. Do not dry it artificially with a heater. Next morning the paper will have shrunk tight and be ready to use.

Methods of Watercolour Painting

Practise making large and small washes of watercolour on your paper. Angle your sketch block or mounted paper

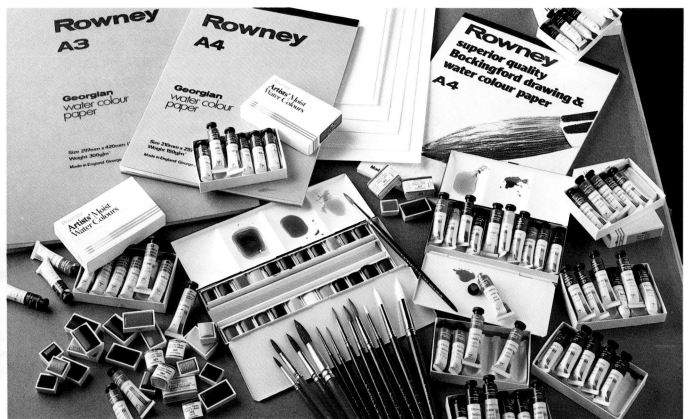

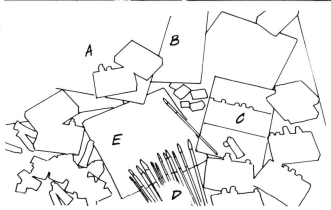

A WATERCOLOUR PADS
B WATERCOLOUR PAPER
C TUBES OF ARTISTS' QUALITY
   WATERCOLOURS
D SABLE, NYLON, MIXED
   HAIR BRUSHES
E PANS OF ARTISTS' MOIST
   WATERCOLOURS

slightly towards you so that the wash will flow downwards easily. Dampen the paper first with clean water, and then with a brushful of colour already mixed in your palette, start at the top left-hand corner and work across and down the paper until the area you want to paint with the wash is completely filled. If necessary, replenish your brush as you go. If you mix a generous quantity of colour in the palette there should not be any change of colour and in this way you can ensure an even wash. If you want a darker tone of the same colour, another wash painted over the first will give a richer shade. This can be done while the first wash is still wet. For a graded wash of colour, add more clean water to the mix in your palette so that the colour will become paler when added to the wash already on your paper. It is best not to add white to watercolours to create lighter shades. Instead, add more water and in this way you can retain the brightness of the original colour. White paint tends to make the colour appear cloudy and less pure.

If pure white is wanted on your picture leave this area unpainted, letting the paper show through, or carefully lift the colour out with a sponge or tissue while the paint is still wet. As I said, a watercolour can be made darker by going over it a second time, but once on your paper it is not so easy to make it lighter. It is here that you can avoid mistakes by thinking ahead.

The 'wet-into-wet' technique of adding more wet paint into an already wet area of paint on the paper to run together the colours and tones, is a difficult method to control. However, it is highly effective for creating atmosphere in skies, distance, horizon and portraying mist or rain and is, therefore, worth practising. For the dry brush technique, fill your brush with colour, wipe or blot off the excess water on a tissue or blotting paper and then drag the brush across the area to be painted so that a broken, stippled effect is created. This is a useful method for painting dappling on horses, or a mane or tail flying in the wind.

EXERCISE ONE
CALVES
IN CHARCOAL

Having just discussed the different uses and potential of the four mediums I generally work in, it will be helpful to describe specific exercises executed in each of these four mediums.

Near my house is a lovely Cotswold farm which was originally a wool mill powered by the Painswick Brook. Apart from its fascinating stone buildings and beautiful rural setting, the farm provides a seemingly unending supply of charming calves from its fine herd of cattle. The kind owners allow me to sketch and take my students there to draw and paint whenever I like, and the enchanting calves make wonderful models. As soon as possible they are weaned from their mothers and taken into the byres where they have warmth and protection on straw-covered floors with plenty of room to move about. Some of the buildings are divided with partitions to make smaller areas and in these you find a few calves huddled together. For the artist these conditions are ideal, as the animals cannot move very far and you can lean against the walled partitions or sit on a straw bale under cover and in relative comfort with your sketchbook.

Calves are easily startled, so when you are painting them don't make sudden movements. Being very inquisitive

animals, when they are used to you being there, they will soon come crowding up to try to lick the charcoal or nibble the edge of the sketchbook. The light in the byre is often dim, but there are subtle tones in the walls, straw, timbered low roof, and the wooden partitions between the stalls. On a summer's day, the sunlight shafts through causing shimmering here and there. The colours of the calves make contrasting patterns in this setting.

One of the first things that strike you when starting to draw or paint calves is their solid and compact forms. Their bodies lack sharp corners or straight lines and everything about them seems to softly curve. The only things which are fairly straight are their long eyelashes, not curling up as one might imagine but jutting out at an angle. Their little cloven hooves are generally pale cream or grey and gently rounded. When drawing calves you will find that their shape and proportion are quite easy to see if you conform to certain basic rules (see also pages 14-15 on Shape and Proportion). Here are a few guidelines which may be of help to you.

With each of the calves shown on these pages, you will notice that the body, legs and head fit into an elongated egg shape. But the head, when seen full on, is the shape of a diamond, with the top and base flattened. The ears come out at right angles from either side of the flattened top. Being only babies, the heads are larger in proportion to the rest of their bodies than those of cows. The measurement down the length of the ear is slightly less than the width between the eyes. The width of the muzzle fits roughly twice across the space between the eyes. Measuring down the head, from the top of the poll to the base of the muzzle, the length of the ear will fit about two and a quarter times. Naturally this varies with the angle of the ears, and depends on whether they are bent forward or back. You will see that they jut out sideways, and do not stand up like those of a horse or donkey. This also applies to sheep, goats and deer. Notice, too, that the eyes are set on the outer edges of the skull, and the nostrils, like two inverted commas, face into each other near the outer edges of the nose.

Try to vary the positions of the animals you draw and paint. It would be dull to have them all in similar attitudes or poses if you were making a group. Of course, if they are in a byre they will spend a lot of time standing together, and if there is hay in the manger they will face towards it. Delightful groupings can be made when the calves are standing with wisps of hay being chewed and pulled from

the heap. They also spend a lot of time with their backs
towards you and this position will require you to take into
account foreshortening, as the head will look smaller from
this angle (see pages 16-17).

I used charcoal for all these drawings of the calves. You
can use ordinary willow charcoal in sticks or charcoal
pencils. If you should want to rub out, use a kneadable
putty rubber. Unless it is vital to remove a wrong line I
generally leave it. Extra lines often give character to a
sketch. I find a sketchbook of white cartridge paper best
for charcoal work. Although it may seem wasteful, it is
advisable to use only one side of the paper when using a
sketchbook. If you don't have a spray fixative with you
then your drawings are less likely to smudge if there is a
plain sheet of paper on top of them when you have to close
the sketchbook. Do try and fix your charcoal and pastel
drawings as soon as you get home.

EXERCISE TWO
PIGS
IN PASTEL

It must have been the hottest day of the year when I decided to make the preliminary sketches of the pigs illustrated here. It had taken me weeks to find a farmer who had a sow who had just farrowed. Piglets are most appealing when they are very small, so I had to try and sketch them only a few days after they were born.

With my largest sketchbook in hand, and a selection of charcoal, loose pastels and Conté crayons, I set off for the farm on the kind invitation of the owner. Even five days after the piglets' birth it was still necessary to be very quiet as there was the danger that the mother might take fright and lie on them. The shed was stiflingly hot because the heaters were constantly on to protect the piglets from draughts. Baby animals need enclosed spaces which are warm and dimly lit, so at first it was not easy to see the piglets snoozing in a heap in the straw after a satisfying meal from mum, but gradually my eyes adjusted to the light. Fortunately, I had taken the precaution of wearing my oldest clothes and a head covering. In the heat the strong smell of the shed and its inmates permeated everything. I could even taste it!

The edge of the stall was of a handy height on which to lean my sketchbook and, with a charcoal stick rather than a charcoal pencil, I started to sketch the general shape of the group of piglets. Speed was essential because, although

they seemed to be asleep, every time I looked up from my drawing one of them had moved! Here there was advantage in numbers as a position was generally duplicated by another piglet. Once I'd sketched in the basic form of the group, I then started to concentrate on individual piglets. Each had its own personality. One, a bit larger than the others, found a comfortable place on its mother's back while the little runt of the litter sat disconsolately against the sow's foreleg while brothers and sisters snuggled comfortably in a heap against her hindquarters and body.

I made a separate drawing of the sow. The texture of her skin with its long white hairs emphasized the strength of the great muscular body. The ears had a shell-like quality of folds and curves, and little veins showed through in places. The nose ended with several wrinkles, and the front of it, where the nostrils were, was like a movable disc which swivelled back and forth as she sniffed the hot air.

Composition
It is one thing to make sketches, but quite another to sort out from those preliminary sketches a suitable combination and arrange them to make a pleasing composition for a finished picture. Scattered drawings, however good, have little impact in a painting unless a good deal of thought has gone into grouping them to make a unified whole. For

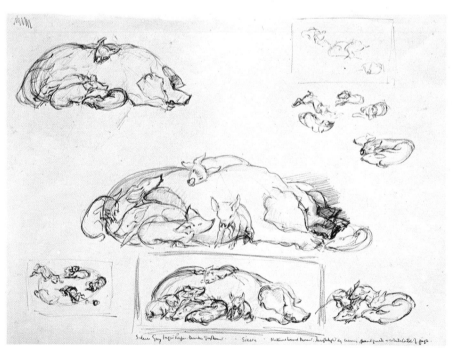

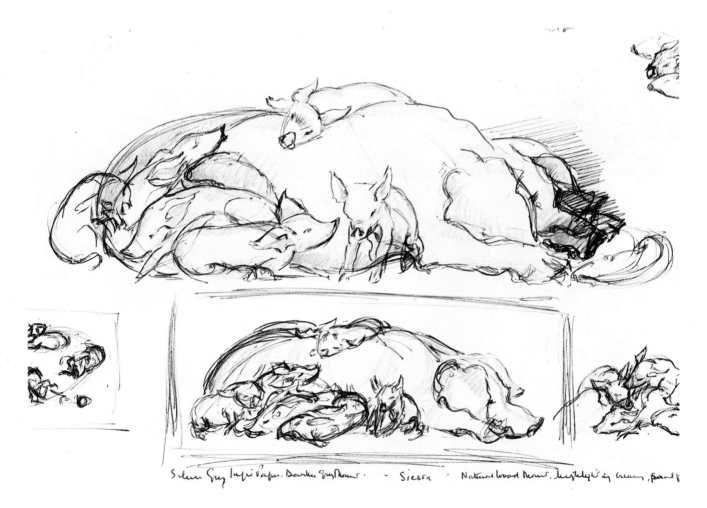

Silver Grey Ingri Paper. Darker Grey Tones. — Siesta. Natural wood tones. lightly in greens, pearl &

example, if this group consists solely of curved shapes it will look too soft so, to break this, at least one upright angular form should be introduced to give impact to the composition. With this in mind I experimented with several different groupings of the piglets against the sow's body but finally put the largest piglet across her back to break that long curve and lead the eye down towards the group of piglets below. I thought of the little runt of the litter. His upright position with his straight little forelegs pushing back against the sow's side was just what I needed for my angular shape. As you can see from the sketches on these pages, I tried various arrangements and ideas before I arrived at my final choice. This is very important when planning a complicated painting and I cannot stress it enough. I altered the positioning of the piglets several times before I was satisfied. The drawing of the sow across the top with the group of piglets beneath (on page 27) was the sketch I originally drew on location in the shed. The drawing was outlined in charcoal and partially filled in with sanguine Conté.

In the close-up of the runt of the litter (this page) you can see how he is placed against the sow's side. Notice how he is slightly knock-kneed and, when drowsy, his eyes became elongated slits. When small, piglets' ears are erect so you can see the detail of the inside formation. The nose is not so pronounced as in an adult, and the head seems far too big for the body. Most babies, whether humans or animals, often give this impression but here it is exaggerated by the foreshortening of his position. Notice, too, the little cloven hooves. All these features are important and you should train yourself to be observant of such details.

I used white Conté to indicate the long white hairs on the sow and for the underlying thick skin over heavy muscle I used the side of a 12mm ($\frac{1}{2}$in) length of broken pastel, Rose Madder Tint 0. The darker areas were done with Burnt Sienna Tint 2; sanguine Conté was used for the very dark tones; and the darkest of all were drawn in with delicate strokes of soft black charcoal pencil.

I gave a great deal of thought to the choice of paper: its weight, texture and colour. I finally decided to use a medium-weight stone-coloured Ingres paper. The tones of the sow and piglets showed up well on this colour background. Remember to think in advance about your background colour as it is important.

Before starting, I padded my drawing board with about 10 sheets of newspaper to make a soft backing for the pastel paper, then carefully pinned it to the board with drawing pins, making sure that it was quite taut. You could, of course, use any kind of scrap paper for backing. Next, with a 6B pencil I very lightly drew in the whole composition

that I had decided upon in my preliminary sketches. Only when I was quite sure that the drawing was correct did I move on to the next stage. With a finely sharpened black charcoal pencil I lightly drew over the pencil outline. Any mistakes at this stage could have been taken out with a putty rubber by gently lifting off the wrong line. I find this method of going over a faint pencil outline more satisfactory than using a tracing which is apt to lose something of the original drawing.

Where a shadow was cast, say under the sow's foreleg and ear, or where it overlapped the shoulder and front leg, I darkened the line by giving more pressure to the stroke. Where light fell on an upper surface, like the top of the piglets' backs or the sow's ear, I used less pressure and this produced a fainter line.

The next stage was to fill in the shape of the animals. I broke a white Conté to about 12mm ($\frac{1}{2}$in) and using the side of it broadly swept in the shape of the sow's body with curves following the shape of the general form and the underlying muscles. I emphasized with white Conté where the light caught the upper surfaces: a wrinkle on her nose, the upper curve of the nearside ear and down its flap and the top of the hindquarters. I did the same thing with the piglets. Then I used the black charcoal pencil, and with

very fine lines drew in the shadows beneath the sow's ears where the ears stand away from the head, and also where the group of piglets were leaning against her side. Next, I added some colour with sanguine Conté under and on the surfaces of the sow's ears. Here the tiny red veins were lightly detailed with the same colour Conté. The sanguine Conté was also used in the darker coloured areas on the piglets. Inside the ears of the runt, under his tummy, and any places which needed a deeper colour I used Burnt Sienna Tint 2 pastel in strokes following the body contours. I used Rose Madder Tint 0 for the lightest colour tones and the basic stone-coloured paper was left uncovered to provide the mid-dark tones. I worked over the whole picture in this way and then stood back to make a final check. I added a highlight here and a touch of dark there until I was satisfied I could take the picture no further.

All that remained was to sign it and hand it over to my framer. I then had the pleasure of seeing it hung in The Pastel Society's Annual Exhibition at The Mall Galleries in London.

EXERCISE THREE
ALSATIAN
IN OILS

I have organized this exercise so that, if you would like to, you can follow it step-by-step. But do read through the whole exercise before you start.

If you look at the first sketch of Cass the Alsatian (**fig. 10**), you will notice that he looks rather disgruntled and cross. In fact he was bored! As his owners did not want him to look like this, alterations had to be made before I did the final drawing on to the canvas for the portrait. To make him look more alert I made the ears prick up and brought them closer together. I also raised the upper eyelids, thus giving him a kinder expression and brought his tail closer to his hindquarters so that his thick hair was shown to advantage. In fact I made his whole pose more

alert. This kind of thing is hard to do when you are a beginner and it takes years of practice but if you study **figs. 10** and **15** carefully you will see how I have altered his expression.

I chose a medium-grained canvas paper size 76 × 51cm (30 × 20in) and, to make it easier to achieve the correct proportions for the dog, I divided the canvas into rectangles by drawing a horizontal and a perpendicular line at the centre of the picture. I went on to make further equal divisions (**fig. 11**). With a more complicated subject I would have made more divisions on the canvas. The central horizontal and perpendicular lines divide the dog's body in half, with the ears, forehead, shoulders, rib cage and top

Fig. 10

of the hindquarters above the central horizontal line, while the lower part of the head, the eyes, stomach and lower quarters and tail come below this line. Check with **fig. 10** and you will see what I mean.

It is a simple matter now to draw the different parts of the dog in these boxes and thus keep everything in proportion. Drawing a boxed framework like this also helps you to keep a space at either side and above and below the dog. It is very important to have the subject placed correctly on the canvas.

If you like, you can sketch out the initial drawing lightly on to the canvas with a stick of willow charcoal, sweeping off any mistakes you may make with a clean brush, rag or tissue. I did my painting straight off with a No. 5 flat hog bristle brush using Burnt Umber diluted with turpentine. This makes the paint thinner and so it flows more easily and can be wiped off in case of error. Remember, if you sketch out your first drawing with charcoal you will have to go over it again with Burnt Umber to fix it.

The colours I used for **fig. 12** were arranged on my mixing palette from left to right: Ivory Black, Cobalt Blue, Viridian, Yellow Ochre, Naples Yellow and a large squeeze of Titanium White. (White is used in the mixing of most colour tones so you will need plenty.) Then Cadmium Yellow Deep, Burnt Umber and Crimson Alizarin. This is quite a restricted palette but from these basic colours you can mix all the tones necessary for painting animals. I find that it always helps to arrange the colours on your palette in the same order every time to prevent confusion.

You will also need a medium to thin the paints which makes them easier to work. Generally this is a mixture of equal parts of turpentine and linseed oil. Keep this in one half of your double dipper (do not overfill it). In the other half you should have turpentine for cleaning your brushes. I always use a palette knife rather than a brush to mix my paints.

Having drawn in the initial outline of the dog with Burnt Umber you will then need to strengthen this outline with Ivory Black before going on to the next phase, which is blocking in the shapes of the dog's markings. Study **fig. 12** carefully, and then proceed. The markings on the Alsatian are black, so, with a No. 6 flat nylon brush and a mix of Ivory Black and turpentine lightly paint in the dark areas. Where grey is needed, for instance on the ears, shoulders and highlights on the nose and rib cage, add White to the Black mix. We now move on to the pale brown and cream areas. Mix Naples Yellow and White on your palette and then, with a clean brush, thinly paint in all the pale brown parts of the dog. Add more White to this mixture for the cream areas. For the deepest tones on the hindquarters, hind legs and tail root, use Naples Yellow undiluted. Apply the same colour, but thinned with turpentine, on the dark areas of the head, ears, shoulders and elbow. For greater impact, place a thin mix of Black between the front and hind legs and along the base of the stomach. Then with the same colour carefully draw in the nose. Notice that this

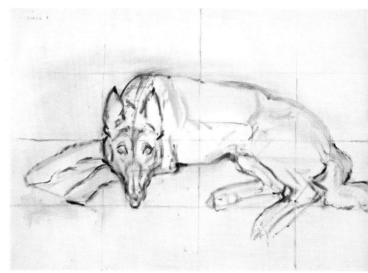

Fig. 11

Fig. 12

Fig. 13

Fig. 14

work over the background as advised. If you look at **fig. 13** you will see that the background is lighter in tone at the extremities but darker where the dog is lying as this helps to indicate shadow. For these darker tones add more Burnt Umber and a little Ivory Black to the original background mix.

Going back to the dog itself you need to fill in some more colour and details. When painting the inside of the ears add more White, a touch of Crimson Alizarin and Burnt Umber to make a soft pink. Darken the outer edges of the ears with Ivory Black, blending down into the grey of the ear.

Great care is needed to paint the eyes so I will take you through this in detail, for the whole liveliness of the picture depends on their expression.

Carefully examine the detail of the face in **fig. 14**. Using a Rowney No. 6 Sable brush Series 133 moistened in medium and with Ivory Black, draw in the upper lid and down the inner side of the eye outlining the tear duct and the slightly dark area below it. Then paint the outer edges of the eye and the shadow area leading up towards the outer base of the ear. Then draw in the shape of the eyeball, but notice that the top is shadowed by the upper eyelid. Next paint the pupil and fill it in. With a similar clean brush, place a dab of White at the top of the eyeball as the highlight, dragging the brush downwards leaving a slightly jagged edge where it blends into the dark area of the pupil. Using another clean brush, paint in the rich brown of the eyeball. For this mix use Burnt Umber with a little Cadmium Yellow Deep and a touch of Crimson Alizarin. Moisten your brush and paint in one curve. Add a little more Cadmium Yellow Deep and lightly touch the brown where the light reflects on the eyeball. Check with **fig. 14** again. Using the same colour but slightly diluted with medium, paint the smooth hairy area round the eye and down into the inner corner against the top of the bridge of the nose. Repeat this method to paint the other eye. Lastly, paint the curve of the eyebrow whisker follicle above each eye. Now you have reached the final stage of putting the finishing touches to your painting (see **fig. 15**). I was fortunate in having a live model, but I hope the stages we have gone through together have been helpful. Compare them carefully with my finished painting and you will see if there is much more to do to your own picture. The background has still to be completed and you do this using the same colour mixes, brushes and method as earlier in the painting. Use the same short strokes working methodically over the whole area, so that no canvas is left uncovered. This is really an abstract background, made up of most of the colours used to paint the dog so that there is harmony in the painting.

You will notice in my final painting that I have softened the edges of the dog's colours and markings. To paint in the rougher areas of the dog's coat you must apply the paint with thick sweeping strokes following the direction of hair growth. This *impasto* treatment is also used for the

is foreshortened, so that the nostrils show only as two small dots. Draw a thinner mix of Black across the shadowed base of the nose, just allowing the nostrils to show through faintly. Only indicate the outline of the eyes at this stage.

The background must now be filled in around the dog (see **fig. 13**). This is done with short strokes of the brush always working outwards and away from the animal with quite thick paint. I find this method gives a more sparkling effect than applying a smooth surface of paint.

For the background colour, place White on your palette, add Cobalt Blue and a little Viridian, then Yellow Ochre and Burnt Umber and mix it all together with your palette knife. The medium for moistening the brush from now onwards should be equal parts of turpentine and linseed oil. The linseed oil adds a richness to the paint. If you continue to use only turpentine as a medium in the later stages of the painting the paint will end up looking too thin and dried out.

The brush I chose for the background was No. 6 Rowney filbert-shaped Nylon Series 220. With the above mix,

Fig. 15

ruff of hair on either side of the face and the thick tail hair.

For highlights on the coat, for example on the rib cage, a smoother appearance is needed and you achieve this by using more medium in the mixture so the paint blends evenly on the surface area. Check the direction of the light source and strengthen the resulting shadows by darkening the existing colours. In my painting this occurs on the right side of the head, on the elbow, tail and on the hind legs. Use a darker tone of the same colours originally mixed for these areas. Paint in the paw pads with grey for their highlights toning down to the darkest shadows with Ivory Black.

Small details, such as toe-nails, need careful attention. Using a No. 6 sable brush, paint the pale cream on the soft paw pads and then the grey, made as before from White with Black added, which subtly changes tone to rich black in the deepest shadows. For the toe-nails use a pale cream (made by mixing White and a little Naples Yellow) and dark Burnt Umber, toning to black underneath. When you put the finishing touches to the muzzle, use a thin blend of Naples Yellow and White, toned down with Burnt Umber. Finally paint in the nose, toning the highlight of grey with a little Ivory Black. I always find that it is good to leave the finished painting for at least a few hours and then come back and look at it carefully. You will be able to observe any little unfinished details much more clearly after a break, and I do hope you are pleased with your finished painting.

Fig. 16

Fig. 17

EXERCISE FOUR
CAT
IN WATERCOLOUR

The preliminary drawing (fig. 16) of Soapy the cat was made on Saunders rough surface paper with an HB pencil. As you can see, this is a complete drawing in itself with details of his markings. However, I later decided to carry this drawing further and make it into a watercolour painting because the cat's colouring was so attractive. This is where it is so useful to take colour notes when sketching. Even if you want the drawing to be complete in itself, you never know when you might want to make a painting of such a drawing.

Only four colours were used in this painting as I wanted to keep it simple and no more were needed to portray Soapy's colours. I used Payne's Grey, Burnt Umber, Cadmium Yellow, and Indian Red; and two brushes, Rowney Nylon Series 270 Nos. 8 and 12. You can see how these four colours were mixed in the simple colour chart in fig. 18.

To paint fig. 17 I used a No. 12 brush and made a generous mix of Payne's Grey and Burnt Umber on my palette with plenty of water. I painted a dark wash of this along the cat's shoulder and down between the curled paw and the side of the left ear. Then I took it up over the back and down over the hindquarters and along the outer side of the tail as far as the cat's muzzle. I also used this colour at the top of the neck just behind the head and in-between the ears. When using watercolour in the preliminary stages you must use plenty of water to keep the wash flowing and prevent hard edges forming. Remember to keep your board tilted so that you can control the direction of the wash.

I then changed to a No. 8 brush and made a mix of Cadmium Yellow and Indian Red as shown in the colour chart (fig. 18) and I used this wash to paint the pale brown pattern on the body, paws and head. I added more Indian Red to the wet colour and used it for the left cheek, above the eyes, and on the bend of the hind leg. Soapy's pale-brown markings were richer with more yellow along the inner length of his tail so I strengthened these areas with more Cadmium Yellow. Using the tip of the brush and a dip of Indian Red I drew in the outline of the eyeballs, the eyes, the nose and the chin.

For the finished painting (fig. 19) I changed back to a No. 12 brush and made another rich mix of Payne's Grey and Burnt Umber and with a well-loaded brush I painted in the dark markings on the body, shoulders and head. Using the tip of the brush and an even richer addition of both colours to the mix, I drew in the ears and then strengthened the dark areas between the ears and forehead

CADMIUM INDIAN   PAYNE'S BURNT
YELLOW RED   GREY   UMBER

Fig. 18

Fig. 19

and along the edge of the bent hind leg.

Next, I made a good rich mix of Cadmium Yellow and Indian Red and ran this into the previous yellow wash along the tail, shoulders and on the bend of the hind leg. I worked more of this rich tone on the forehead adding a little more Cadmium Yellow on the face above the eyes, along the bridge of the nose, inside the ears and into the lighter markings on the tail.

For the background I made a large pool of Payne's Grey and Burnt Umber which I painted all round the outline of the cat. I then made a second wash of the same colours and overlapped the first wash, allowing an edge to form halfway up across either side of the body to differentiate between the background and the area on which the cat is lying. I then ran a third wash from the base of his back and beneath him to just under his paws. When painting abstract backgrounds like this in watercolour you must always use plenty of water and allow each wash to run slightly into the next so that there are no harsh edges and it all blends together harmoniously.

When the background was finished I strengthened the eyes by using another mix of Indian Red and Burnt Umber painted on with the very tip of the brush. The areas around the nose and mouth also needed strengthening in the same way and, finally, I drew the whiskers in very delicately with Payne's Grey and Burnt Umber.

PAINTING HAIR AND FUR

A good animal portrait must incorporate all the different aspects of the animal's appearance to make a finished likeness and therefore painting hair and fur is an important skill to learn. Much of the animal's character and shape will be lost if you do not properly show whether its coat is rough or smooth, long or short or a mixture. Look closely at your subject, and make notes around your preliminary sketches. Look also at the areas where the fur lies in different directions. This is often a clue to the anatomy beneath. If practicable you should gently feel the animal's fur for the muscle and bone structure which it hides. You will then understand the reason why the fur lies as it does.

The effects of light and shadow play an important part in depicting hair and fur. They show whether a coat is glossy or matt and also show the curvature of the body. Generally, shadows form underneath the body and in folds and creases in the hair. The light correspondingly touches the smoother and more exposed surfaces, hence the term 'highlight'.

There are some similarities in the way you should tackle the problems of hair and fur in whichever medium you use. But there are distinct differences too, particularly in painting the undercoat, so we shall look at pastels, watercolours and oils separately.

Pastels

Pastels are very useful and flexible for indicating the different types of hair and fur. You can use the side of the pastel for a light sweep of colour which is suitable for smooth-haired animals (see Siamese cats in pastel on pages 54–57). More pressure will give a denser impression suitable for rougher coats. The sharp edge of a pastel stick can be used to show individual hairs and whiskers.

Choose a colour of paper compatible with the colours of your subject because very often the paper will show through your finished portrait in a few places. This is quite acceptable and indeed, the paper will act as an additional colour in your painting rather than remain a separate background (see the pigs on pages 26–29).

Your first approach should always be to apply just a few colours in broad patches as an undercoat. Where you see one predominant body colour, e.g. reddish-brown, use two similar pastel colours, such as Burnt Sienna and Rose Madder, together in different amounts. This will also impart richness and depth to the undercoat, making it easier to put details in later. These colours should not be too light or too dark. Even at this stage you should make the pastel

Fig. 20   Pen and ink with watercolour on Ingres paper

follow the direction of the fur, lifting the pastel and changing direction as the fur changes on the animal's body. Shadow should be indicated in a slightly darker colour, leaving the strongest darks to be added later.

If the animal's coat is glossy, for example like a horse's, you may wish to add a few broad highlights and then blend each colour in gently with your finger. In this way the colours will not blur completely into each other, but the edges between the colours will be less distinct and more in keeping with a smooth and glossy coat.

Generally, the more shaggy the fur is, the more detail you are likely to put in. You can use a contrasting colour or repeat an earlier colour using greater pressure to show clumps or tufts of hair and draw thin lines for individual hairs. Follow the direction of the hair once again. Do not use too much of your darkest and lightest colours: keep them for real extremes. Draw individual whiskers very finely, especially on the face and head and do not draw in too many.

Watercolours

A successful animal portrait in watercolour should be clear and fresh-looking without too much detail. However, as watercolours are transparent you should try and visualize the successive stages before starting. Mistakes cannot be easily rectified and your first marks will still be visible even when later washes have been applied over them.

Look at the animal you are painting in terms of light and dark. You should always tackle the largest parts first. Mix your colours on your palette with plenty of water – it is better to be too light than too dark at this stage. Leave dry

Fig. 21 Watercolour on white Saunders rough paper

any areas that are to remain white, for example the blaze on a horse's forehead. Apply colour in broad sweeps with a fully-loaded sable brush. The brush should be large enough to wash over the animal-shape in one or two passes, but not so large that it cannot be controlled at the edges.

Block in the main areas of shadow in the same way using a darker colour. The undercoat should then be allowed to dry. With slightly thicker paint and using a sable brush, break each area up into a few similar colours and apply these in large sweeping strokes which again follow the lie of the fur and contours of the body. Where necessary these can be blended with a rag, dry brush or your finger. It is important here to capture the variety of colour without making the animal seem like a patchwork of unrelated colours.

Where the fur is smoothest the colour should not be applied too energetically otherwise the shape and detail could be lost. This is especially true on the head and face. Here the small pouches under the eyes and the shape of the muzzle are created by curved brush strokes applied with a sharp, controlled, wrist action. Strong contrasting colours should not be used too freely, but may ultimately be required around the eyes and nose to give them their shape. Use a fine sable brush for this.

If you wish to create the impression of a fairly shaggy, uneven coat you can apply the second wash before the first has dried. This gives a pleasing impressionistic effect rather than an absolutely precise outline. Alternatively, wait until the first wash is dry and then, with the same colour, apply a second wash to those areas which are to be darker. Follow the direction of the fur and the curve of the body. Where the body has received only one wash it will appear glossier because the paper's whiteness is visible through the colour washes. Subsequent stages are done in the same way, but you should not apply too many washes over each other. If you feel that the colour should vary slightly in places, a thin wash of a new, nearly pure colour will be muted when placed over a duller mixture.

Details such as individual whiskers are applied lightly once the washes are dry. A fine sable brush is best for this. Alternatively, a pen dipped in ink of a suitable colour can be used. The colour employed should not contrast too sharply with the wash colour: pure white or black are too strong.

You might find it useful here to compare my two water-colour paintings of Dinky the cat. In **fig. 20** you will see how the cat's outline has been picked out in black pen as well as the nose, ears and eyes. I have tried to portray Dinky's coat and the sleeker fur on her head and paws in contrast to the rest. In **fig. 21** I concentrated on the overall fluffy effect of her dense fur.

Oils

Oil colour as a medium is very well-suited for depicting the texture of fur as it can be put on thickly to give the impression of a third dimension to the painting. Pastel and watercolour, are, by and large, flat and two-dimensional, but oil can be built up layer by layer and streaked and ridged just like the animal's hair itself. I used this technique, called *impasto*, when painting Cass the Alsatian (see pages 30–33).

Initially, you should block in an undercoat in thin paint of approximately the correct fur colour. The paint should be thinned with turpentine at this stage and used with a medium-sized nylon brush (perhaps a No. 4) to draw the animal's outline. The outline should then be filled in by rubbing it with a rag dipped in the diluted colour. Alternatively, a flat-ended hog bristle brush can be used. This first coat should not be applied too smoothly, but should, once again, broadly follow the main directional sweeps of the hair.

Larger highlights on fur should be added in a lighter colour than the main body colour and should be diluted with turpentine. When blended in, these lighter highlights make the coat look smooth and glossy.

But where the coat is rough you will need to apply the paint more thickly. On an animal such as the St Bernard (page 17) several layers of paint may need to be built up. A palette knife can be used quite effectively for this, but you will have more control with a medium-sized hog bristle or nylon brush. Remember to follow the direction of the fur. Paint applied *impasto* in this way can give your portrait real substance and depth with the ridges of *impasto* creating their own subtle shadows.

If necessary, individual hairs can now be overpainted more thinly in a slightly contrasting colour or tone using a fine sable brush. But don't overdo either *impasto* or the finer details.

PAINTING HAIR AND FUR
LITTLE WHITE DOG
IN OILS

For the first sketches of the little white dog I used a black medium-tip ballpoint pen, and wrote notes around the sketch as 'memory joggers' (see **fig. 22**). This little dog was very lively, so I had to work extremely fast. He came to my studio for me to make the first drawings but I thought for the final painting I would prefer him to be sitting on the grass outside. He was very alert and I made some observations of his characteristics. He had one raised 'fly-away' ear, which was white, while the other, which was folded down neatly, was black. Both ears were of a smooth, silky texture, very different from the rough hair over the rest of his body. He had a very shiny little black nose reminiscent of an old-fashioned black, boot button! His nostrils were well defined and his mouth was clear cut but with short hairs falling down across the upper lip. His front legs were slightly knock-kneed and all his toe-nails were neat and well-shaped. The shaggy hair on his body became smoother as it went down his legs to the paws. His tail was held erect and wagged fast and frequently. This look of cheeky alertness was typical of him and I wanted to capture in my painting the feeling that he might jump up at any moment and run off to play.

Before you start any drawing or painting of a shaggy dog, do talk to the owner beforehand and make sure that they will not decide that the dog looks untidy and have its fur trimmed in-between 'sittings'! This has happened to me, and it is most frustrating, as naturally the whole look and expression of the animal is changed. In fact, you have to start all over again.

As I have said earlier in this section it is difficult with rough-coated animals to know what their bone structure is like so you must try to imagine just where the muscles and bones are under all that hair. If you are working from a live model, stroke it gently and you will feel the bone structure beneath. It is very important to look for anything which will help to give you an indication of the body formation. One point to note is that generally the direction of hair growth follows the body shape.

Down the bridge of the little dog's nose there is a definite parting and the hair grows away in opposite directions. It falls in long strands over the cheeks and upper part of the muzzle. The seeming confusion of hair on the top of his head does flow into definite patterns above, around and behind each ear, whereas below the ears, at the back of the head, the nape of the neck and down the shoulders, the hair is slightly shorter. His moustache grows down from either side around his shiny, black nose. Along the centre

of the dog's back there is a distinct parting which runs right down to the tail root. It is important to note all these things about fur and texture when you are doing your preliminary sketches.

For this painting I chose a medium textured canvas board 51 × 41cm (20 × 16in). I used the basic palette as described on pages 20-21 and the following brushes: Series 220 Nylon Nos. 8 and 6, Series 133 Sable Nos. 6 and 4.

In **fig. 23** I copied the pen sketch from my sketchbook on to the board using a Series 220 Nylon No. 6 brush and Burnt Umber thinned with turpentine.

As this was a very small dog I decided to position it on the canvas in such a way that the viewer is looking slightly down on it, which helps to emphasize how small the dog is. Having carefully drawn the animal's outline and the shape of the eyes I put the dark areas in on his one black ear and its shadow beneath, the inside of the white ear, a bit under his nose, and on the lower lip and under his chin. Next the areas of background shadows behind and beneath the dog were rubbed in with a rag dipped in a thin solution of Black paint and turpentine.

As the dog was white I decided on a darker background to make him stand out. For **fig. 24** I first made a mix of white to which I added Viridian and Yellow Ochre. Using a Series 220 Nylon No. 8 brush moistened in equal parts of turpentine and linseed oil I started work in the upper left-hand corner of the canvas and gradually moved across the background of the picture using short, dabbing strokes. I added a little more Yellow Ochre where I painted down and around the tail. This colour mixture was taken down the right side of the picture and right round to the other side of the dog, but always leaving some canvas showing through to give an effect of lightness and sparkle. I did not fill in all the background at this stage of the painting, but turned back to the dog itself to paint in the darker tones of its fur. For these I added to the original mixture of Ivory Black and turpentine, a little Cobalt Blue and Viridian. With a clean No. 8 nylon brush I painted in the darker tones around the raised white ear and down the side of the head as well as the shadows beneath and between the front legs and under the body leading up to the hindquarters.

I then mixed Cobalt Blue with Cadmium Yellow and a little White and worked down the right side of the canvas and around the dog and along the base of the picture to fill in the rest of the background. If your colour seems too strong, add a little more White until you have the desired tone of green. Where the darker and lighter tones meet in the

Fig. 22

background I blended them together with short, dabbing strokes, so that there were no hard edges. I used two No. 6 nylon brushes, one for the darker tones and one for the lighter. You should blend the dark tones into the light very gradually to get the same effect as in my painting (fig. 26).

Going back to the dog, a smooth underpainting of white was applied on which the impression of rough fur can be built up layer by layer (fig. 26). With a Series 220 Nylon No. 6 brush, sparingly moistened with medium but well loaded with White, I painted the left ear. I worked all over the white areas of the dog always applying the paint thickly. I then painted the highlight on the edge of the flap of the black ear. Some of the initial guidelines of the original drawing could be overpainted here as there should be no hard edge showing around the dog in this final stage. The

dark tones which occur just above the root of the tail and extend along the right side of the hindquarters, haunch, stomach and under the chin were filled in by adding a little Burnt Umber and Black to the white mixture. These darker tones also need to be where the upper part of the front leg joins the chest and at the joint of the front paws and upper legs.

I then painted the dark ear in detail. Notice that it is made up of tones of black and grey, with the white highlight on the flap blended into the black of the outer ear. The tone inside the ear is an even darker grey. A touch of Crimson Alizarin with Burnt Umber and White mixed to make a pink flesh tone was applied just under the ear flap. A touch of this skin colour was also painted at the corners of the eyes and above the black at the top of the nose just

Fig. 23

Fig. 24

Fig. 25

where the hair divides. There is also a glimpse of pink between the central toes on each front paw.

I painted the nose with a diluted mix of Black and the medium, while the highlight was a pale grey (see **fig. 25**). I purposely did not paint the highlight white as it would have looked too bright. The outline of the nose and nostrils was painted in Black with a Series 133 Sable No. 6 brush. As always the whole expression of the animal is dependent upon a good portrayal of the eyes. These had already been drawn in so it was just a matter of filling in the details. The whites of this little dog's eyes show very clearly against his brown pupils. These whites were painted with pure White with a Series 133 Sable No. 4 brush moistened with medium. The rich brown pupils were painted next, using a No. 4 sable brush and a mix of Cadmium Yellow, a small amount of Burnt Umber and a touch of Crimson Alizarin. The iris was painted in a curve with Black on a No. 4 sable brush, leaving the highlight clear. I added a touch of White into this highlight. Look closely at the detail of the dog's face to see how I painted his features (**fig. 25**).

Finally, I added the finishing touches to the dog's coat. Using a Series 220 Nylon No. 6 brush loaded with thick White paint (no medium was used to thin this down) I painted on layer after layer following the sweep of the hair growth. This should end up beautifully thick (*impasto*) so you feel that you can practically touch his rough, ragged coat!

JEAN PARKE-WILLIAMS.

PORTRAYING EXPRESSION

In successfully capturing an animal's expression you are bringing a picture to life and so the expression is often the single most important part of your picture. This is true at each stage from the initial drawing to the final touches of colour or shading.

The Eyes

An animal's eyes tell us most about its character or mood and must be drawn very accurately. It can be useful to sketch the eyes and indeed the whole head separately on a larger scale to the rest of the picture in order to grasp the subtle lines which mean so much. Use a sharp pencil or pastel, a fine charcoal stick or a small sable brush to draw the lines clearly. Drawing the same animal in several different moods helps you to understand the slight variations of lines which produce different expressions.

First check the size and position of the eyes in relation to the other features of the head. How far apart are the eyes? Perhaps they are set at a slight angle or V-shape, to the nose. If so, how pronounced is the angle? Then look at the curve of the upper eyelid compared to the lower. If the upper lid is arched the animal may look quizzical, friendly or perhaps sleepy (see **fig. 27**).

In dogs this could be accompanied by drooping jowls beside the mouth and pouches or bags under the eyes, as with the Bassett hounds in **fig. 28**. If the arching is more pronounced the animal might appear to be staring intently at something. On the other hand, a straighter look to the upper lid may make the animal seem wary or even angry. This particularly applies when drawing cats. A concentration of shadow here would enhance the slightly frowning appearance. This is useful if you want to show a cat about to pounce on something which has riveted its attention – for example, a ball of wool. The eyes of a Siamese cat would be set close together and the pupils would appear to point inwards, making the cat look cross-eyed. Remember, too, that cats' pupils dilate in the dark and are just slits in bright light.

An important factor in portraying a dog's expression is the amount of shadow and detail around the eyebrow follicle, situated above each eye.

Also, the more circular a cat's or dog's eyes appear, the franker or more playful the animal looks. This is particularly true of kittens or puppies. Care and accuracy are needed, however, since it is unlikely that the eyes will look perfectly circular. The size of the pupils must also be checked as you don't want the animal to look as though it is staring.

Fig. 27

Not all expressions can be described in human terms such as trusting, affectionate or playful, but all can be depicted, in any animal, by carefully looking at the give-away signs in the shape of the eyes. Showing whether they are round, narrowed, arched or oval-shaped is the first step to capturing an expression.

You must also be accurate in drawing the corners and tear-ducts of each eye to complete the eye shape. Is the tear-duct level with the outer corner or lower than it, so making the eye seem angled or slanted? This simple feature could change the animal's whole expression. Check also that you have created a *pair* of eyes rather than two that don't match. They won't match if one is level and the other slanted, for example, or if one is nearer the nose than the other. However, they may not be perfect replicas of each other since your position in relation to the animal will make the drawing of each eye slightly different.

After the drawing, the next important stage comes in the colouring and shading of the eye and in showing its highlight. Be careful in positioning the highlight and in gauging its intensity as incorrect placing of this highlight will alter the whole expression. It may be altogether too harsh to place a highlight on the pupil in pure white. If you are using white paper you may wish to leave the

Fig. 28

highlight unpainted initially and later paint a pale, transparent wash over the whole eye or shade it very delicately. This would tone it in slightly, but still leave it sufficiently distinct and alive. Alternatively, it may be blended in with the colour of the iris at one side; this too will lessen its harshness. Whether an animal is in bright light or in the shade, whether it is alert or sleepy – all these factors will affect how strong you choose to make the highlight.

Again, remember that the eyes must be treated as a pair, so both highlights will almost certainly be placed and treated in a similar way.

In painting the rest of the eye the choices are the same. It is usually better to paint a few shades of similar colours blended together than to paint one colour which would make the eye look flat and lacking in depth. Here again a transparent overglaze might help. Look at the Alsatian in oils on pages 30-33 and note the way I painted his very expressive eyes.

The Head and Body

Naturally the eyes are of paramount importance in getting an animal's expression right. But there may be pointers in the mouth, nose, ears and elsewhere which would reinforce the expression you have depicted in the eyes. Perhaps you can show a puppy's lopsided grin or the set of its ears. The alert ears of a Doberman would require different treatment from those of a terrier that had one ear erect and the other lying flat. A horse's ears can tell us a lot about how it feels. If they are lying back against its head, with eyes wide and nostrils flaring, it is either afraid or annoyed and should be comforted or left alone to calm down. However, when a horse's ears are pricked forward it means that the horse is alert and inquisitive (see the picture of the mare and foal on page 51).

Having tackled the drawing of the head, look again at the body to see if it mirrors the facial expression in any way. Concentration in the eyes may be supported by tenseness in the body: an action suspended or about to happen. A sleepy animal's whole body will be relaxed and may seem a soft bundle of curved lines and fur.

All of these points are simply a question of careful observation and accurate drawing. Checking relative positions, sizes and angles methodically will eventually produce an instinct in you for what is essential in an animal's expression. There is no point in tackling points of detail elsewhere until you have first attempted to capture the expression. But once you have caught this you can feel confident that you have brought your picture to life.

PORTRAYING EXPRESSION
MY PUPPY TESS
IN PASTEL

Fig. 29

I've had Tess since she was just six weeks old. She was the ideal subject for painting because she was so adorable and I was determined to capture her personality and character in a picture. While playing she would suddenly flop down, her legs and paws at all angles. Using a large sketchbook, I did a number of sketches on each page as she changed position. I talked to keep her attention and she very soon realized that I wanted her to keep still. She learned quickly.

The three drawings on this page (fig. 29) were done with a medium-tip black ballpoint pen and coloured with pastel Yellow Ochre Tint 4. For the darker areas I used sanguine Conté, with Burnt Umber Tint 4 for the eyes and Madder Brown Tint 2 for the protruding tip of her tongue and her paw pads. I planned to make the final pastel painting one of Tess in three completely different poses. After I had done several drawings of her in different positions I grouped them together and rearranged them several times. I finally decided to use one of her lying on her tummy looking soulful; one of her asleep curled up with her paws in a heap and her tongue protruding, and one of her half sitting up. As you will see in the original drawing she had a ball in front of her to show how small she was in proportion to it.

However, despite much arranging and rearranging the drawings did not seem to group well together. So I made myself a mug of coffee and walked round the garden, trying to clear my mind and work out the problem.

Back at the easel I suddenly realized that it was the ball which made everything look wrong. This odd shape was out of keeping with the rest of the forms, so I removed it. However, this presented me with a new problem: Tess's far front paw seemed to lead the eye out and away from the picture. Then I remembered her habit of crossing one paw over the other. It took only a few moments to alter the position of the paw and suddenly it had all fallen into place. This exercise in composition illustrates the importance of preliminary sketching and careful observation. And as I've said before, if something doesn't seem quite right, go away from the painting, do something else and clear your mind, then when you return to the painting you can look at it with a fresh eye and, hopefully, spot the error.

Now for the final painting of Tess (fig. 30). I chose a sheet of medium-thickness Fabriano 160gm² paper, size 50 × 70cm (27½ × 19½in). Using a 4B pencil, I very lightly and carefully drew in the three poses I had decided on, making sure that the drawing and placing of each pose was correct by constantly referring back to my sketches. When building up such a picture, great care must be taken in forming the basic shapes and when using pastel and charcoal you must be very careful not to smudge your work with your hand. Using a finely sharpened black charcoal pencil I went lightly over the 4B pencil guidelines. Now I had to show the contours of the body, which were gradually worked in using the charcoal in fine lines to follow the growth of the hair and show the bone structure and muscle formation underneath. With white Conté I put in the light areas on the back of her head, paws, legs, and the small white feather shape on the back of her neck. The light golden brown markings were filled in with Yellow Ochre pastel Tint 4, and where these tones darkened into shadows, sanguine Conté. The nose in each case was carefully drawn with a sharpened charcoal pencil. In each pose there is a two-toned highlight showing across the top of the nose, and round the nostrils (see **fig. 31**). For the mid-tone I used Cool Grey pastel Tint 4 and for the very light tone, white Conté. I finely sharpened my black charcoal pencil and drew in the shape of the eyes; first the eyeball, and the upper and lower eyelids which slightly overlapped the eyeball above and below. Then I painted a narrow curve of Yellow Ochre pastel Tint 4 around the base to half way up either side of the eyeball.

When drawing the pupil I again used the sharpened black charcoal pencil filling in from the base towards the centre where I left a small area of the basic grey paper uncovered as the highlight. This in turn had a tiny dot of white Conté placed where more light was reflected. Finally, I put a touch of sanguine Conté at the inner corner of the eye, against the tear-duct.

I think a dog's paws are very appealing, and Tess's were particularly so when she was a puppy. Her toes needed careful observation, with special attention given to the drawing of the toe-nails, the way they fitted into their sockets and their delicate creamy-white colour. The pads were smoothly-shaped ovals and the central pad, equivalent to the palm of the human hand, softly curved. Each pad was separated by very short, velvety hair. I painted the pads with Madder Brown Tint 2 and added a touch of white Conté where the light caught them. For the darker areas around her muzzle I drew tiny overlapping lines with black charcoal pencil. The tongue was painted with Madder Brown Tint 2 and I darkened it just under and against the upper lip with a touch of black charcoal pencil.

I worked all three poses more or less together, going from one to the other so that the effect was gradually built up evenly over the whole picture at the same time. In this way you maintain a feeling of unison despite there being three separate poses. I gave the bodies weight and form by using the flat side of a broken black Conté in sweeping curves which followed the shapes of Tess's form. In the dark areas I gave extra depth of tone with Ivory Black pastel slightly pressed (not rubbed in) with the tip of a finger, and then worked over it with a fine line, here and there, of black charcoal pencil.

Fig. 30

Fig. 31

PORTRAYING MOVEMENT

The time will come when you decide you want to capture the likeness of a moving animal in a painting. It could be of a horse trotting, or a dog or cat running. Whatever animal you are trying to show in motion, you should think fairly carefully about how to portray it. A painting is after all flat and still (two-dimensional) so any attempt at capturing something solid and moving will involve some measure of illusion.

Firstly, you must understand how the animal moves. Different animals move in different ways. Their movement also changes according to how fast they are going: for example, a horse's walk involves a different sequence of leg positions to its trot and its gallop. When an animal walks some of its feet will be touching the ground but as it runs or gallops there will be moments when none of its feet are on the ground.

Observe as much of an animal's movement as you can before you start to draw. Then do several quick sketches with a fibre-tip pen, pencil or some other medium which enables you to work swiftly. Don't worry if the sketches are unfinished. You should be able to extract the most important parts from different sketches of similar movements and then combine them into one which should depict the desired movement accurately. Such quick sketches often have a flowing action to them which is part

Polo 41 × 51cm (16 × 20in)

of your instinctive and rapid response to a moving subject. These help create the 'feel' of the action. If you choose to supplement your study of animal movement by looking at photographs and drawings in books do not forget that your original, unfinished sketches from real life may well have captured the essence or illusion of movement and something of them will be needed in your final work. Essentially, a photograph is unselective whereas a drawing selects – even if the decisions and choices made are instinctive. A photograph shows every detail in sharp focus, it freezes the action; a drawing can show the important overall impression and you may choose to eliminate unimportant details which clutter the picture.

If you choose not to aim for the still, frozen image, you will have to decide which details can be suppressed. For instance, is it important to show the ground under the animal's feet? A foot touching the ground may anchor the picture and destroy the sense of movement. It is helpful to suggest the shape of a paw or hoof but it may be unnecessary to show every detail. On the other hand, details will still be needed on the face and head: the eyes will show the animal's personality, the ears may lay back along the head if the animal is moving very fast.

Generally, more detail will be shown in an animal that is walking than in one that is running as fast as it can. For a walking animal the 'frozen image' may be acceptable, and consequently presents fewer problems to the artist.

When portraying fast movement (see *Polo*, this page) hard contrasting colours should be softened and body colours blurred together or streaked slightly. If pencils, pen or pastels are used, shading may be done by lines drawn very close together rather than a solid shadow. In watercolour or oils you can consider leaving the sweep of the brushmarks subtly showing through but they must follow the direction of movement. If you feel technically competent enough, you may endeavour to create a very slight blur of movement, especially around the feet and away from the head. This would be in a softer, lighter version of the body colour with no sharply-defined lines.

The lines of the body should be seen to flow. They should form smooth curves and not be used to sharply define each individual muscle. They may fade slightly on the tail and ankles as they do in the ballpoint pen drawings of the greyhounds on page 47, but need to be strengthened where they are most important – on the spine. A line which is too broken will destroy the movement; but equally a continuous outline may deaden and flatten it. As always it is a question of balance.

A running or galloping animal is an animal of extremes. Its muscles bunch and tense ready to spring, then extend outwards in a leap. This process is repeated continuously. As a greyhound's body tenses the legs bend in under its belly, the spine is arched, the neck and head held up slightly. In the long stride that follows the body straightens, head and front legs extend forward almost touching each other, backlegs extend full stretch behind. At neither

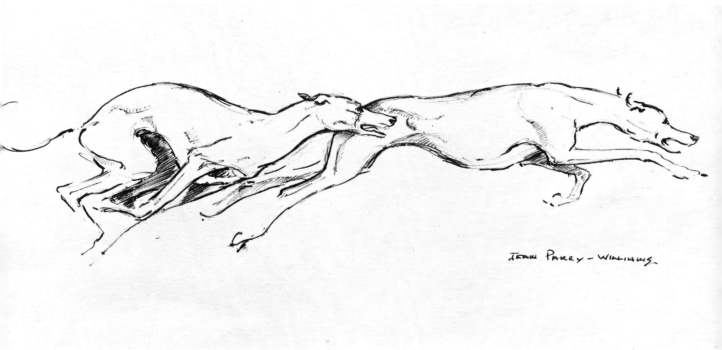

extreme do the feet touch the ground (see my pastel paint-ing of greyhounds racing on page 49). Similar observations can be made for cats, horses, rabbits etc., although each will have its own particular strides, paces and muscle patterns.

At various points between the extremes mentioned the feet do touch down, often in sequence but not in unison. Curiously, it is preferable to draw the front feet touching down at the end of a leap rather than show the rear feet still on the ground at its start. This somehow roots the feet to the spot so that rather than creating an illusion of movement you create one of a sculptured animal on tip-toe reaching out but not moving.

Other things also help to create an illusion of movement. For example, a horse's mane and tail. The mane streams wildly out behind the head and the tail is raised to about 45 degrees when the horse is cantering or galloping. Also, if you are painting a picture of, say, a show-jumping scene, you will need to observe the way a horse's legs tuck under its body as it clears the jumps. Similarly, you will have the position of the rider to examine. Is he or she seated in the saddle, or, when jumping, propelled very slightly out of the saddle? The faster the horse goes, the more the rider leans forward against its neck. Reins will be held tightly and will not be slack. All these points should be carefully noted.

While all drawings of moving animals pose special prob-lems, there are fewer if you are doing a profile. For reasons of dramatic impact or to record a particular observation, you may choose to draw a more complex, front-on view.

Moving animals seen head-on or at a slight angle present all the problems of foreshortening with little of the pred-ictability that a stationary animal might have. For this reason I recommend you be very self-critical in your observations and take nothing for granted. Use photo-graphs as an aid if you wish. The size/comparison method of drawing proportions (see pages 14-15) is a useful tool under these circumstances. Often a large expanse of body will be compressed by foreshortening into a small space in your picture. By comparing it with, say, the head size, you can eliminate any distortion that may make your picture seem ridiculous to someone who is more familiar with the animal than you are. This way of portraying movement is more difficult than doing a profile view and takes time, practice and confidence to perfect – but it will come in the end!

Finally, there is the question of background. Do you want to include one at all? If so, how detailed should it be? A clear, sharp-focus background presumes the time to observe it; in other words it is slightly alien to the idea of speed of movement where details are blurred. Conse-quently, such a background would only be used if the movement was slow because it would have an anchoring effect.

It is clear, then, that depicting movement requires care-ful observation and a knowledge of your subject. Equally it involves artistic judgements of selection and refinement. When these come together successfully into a finished picture the result is one of increased impact and drama and you can feel satisfied with a job well done.

PORTRAYING MOVEMENT
GREYHOUNDS
IN PASTEL

I will now describe to you how I painted in pastel the running greyhounds in my painting, *Running Free*. I first made a quick sketch with black ballpoint pen of a single, racing greyhound (below) showing the outlines of the

jacket and muzzle. Next I drew two hounds wearing racing colours and muzzles, each in a different position with one just ahead of the other (**fig. 32**). This created a feeling of continuity and forward movement which would have been lost if there was a space between the dogs. For this drawing I used black ballpoint pen and coloured pencils. For my final preliminary sketch I drew the two greyhounds in the same position as in the second sketch, but without their racing harnesses.

Then I had to choose a suitable paper. First of all I tried a fawn Ingres paper but this colour did not look right with the silvery grey tones of the hounds, so I decided to use a blue/grey Ingres paper. I planned to have a slightly darker grey mount with a silvered frame.

I pinned the blue/grey Ingres paper to my board and lightly drew in the outline of the animals with a 4B pencil. When I was satisfied that the drawing was correct I sharpened a medium black charcoal pencil and carefully drew over the pencil outline of the hounds again. Before you actually start to paint in pastel it is important to test the

Fig. 32

colour of your pastel on the edge of the paper you have chosen to see how it will look before applying it to your drawing. Pastel can look quite different on various shades of paper. For instance, the Purple Grey Tint 0 has a mauve tone when applied to white paper but on blue/grey Ingres paper it gives just the right impression of the silvery grey of the greyhound's coat. The testing of pastel colours is especially necessary if you are using a shade of paper different to the one that you normally use.

As you can see, both greyhounds have very pale coats (see **fig. 33**). For the rear greyhound I chose a Cool Grey Tint 2 pastel to fill in the main form. I broke the stick in half and using the side, swept in the shapes of the large muscles, along the neck, over the shoulders, the rib cage and along the flank. With the edge of my finger I then smoothed the edges of the applied pastel so that they softly blended into the paper without leaving a hard edge. This helped to give a feeling of solidity to the moving body. Next came the richer half-tones where the form curved in, and for these I used Vandyke Brown Tint 1 and again used the edge of my finger to blend in the colours.

For the leading greyhound I changed to Purple Grey Tint 0. I worked this over the body in the same way that I painted the other dog, again using the tip of my finger to work in the edges of the form. Where the tones became lighter I used the side of a broken piece of Silver White pastel. I varied the effect of light and shade on the charcoal pencil lines by decreasing and increasing the pressure of the stroke. The darkest shaded areas on both hounds were hatched in with the same charcoal pencil, i.e. fine lines drawn very close together. I painted the lightest highlights on both hounds with white Conté.

With the exception of the strengthened black drawing lines, and the dark hatched shadows, the whole picture was worked in very pale tones so that when it was finished, mounted and framed, the effect was a harmonious blend of pale colours.

The impact of the painting lies in the variations of weight in the light and dark charcoal lines, and the rhythm and sweep of the movement of the dogs.

Fig. 33   *Running Free* 41 × 76cm (16 × 30in)

PAINTING BACKGROUNDS

Your success in painting and drawing animals will undoubtedly be enhanced if you understand the importance of viewing your picture as a whole. For every painting you will need to decide whether or not a background is required. If you are sketching an animal, or a group of animals, a background will be needed only in so far as it adds to the information you are collecting in your sketch. Most paintings which are taken beyond the sketch stage will, however, need some form of background to make them complete, even if it is only a suggestion as in the watercolour sketch of horses grazing in a field shown here. This is not just a matter of providing information about the animal's habitat but is important for creating a decorative setting for the painting.

Whichever type of setting you choose, it is wise to echo the colours of the animal in the background around it. If this seems difficult – for example, if you have a brown dog set against a green carpet – it should still be possible to harmonize the two by adding a hint of the brown to the green mixture, but not enough to change it completely. There *may* even be a few hints of a greenish mixture added to the shadows in the dog's fur, but this should not be overdone. A dog painted in warm brown colours would look stark and unreal against a plain white setting; so a warmer-coloured background would improve the overall effect of the picture enormously. Remember that brighter colours are more difficult to harmonize. Most colours in nature are not as pure as the colours of paints and pastels, so it is beneficial for you to mix and tone down your colours if you are aiming at realism and colour harmony in your painting.

Is the animal the most important feature of your painting? If so, it will be detailed and prominent against a suggestion of a background which itself contains very little detail. This is frequently the case if you wish to capture the likeness of a pet or favourite animal in a portrait. For examples see my puppy Tess on pages 44–45 and the little white dog on pages 38–41. If, on the other hand, you are depicting a farmyard scene in which the buildings and farm equipment are as essential to your painting as the animals, you should treat each feature equally and none should be given undue prominence.

Basically, there are three types of background to be considered: outdoor, interior and abstract.

Outdoor Backgrounds

Some typical examples of outdoor settings are: a sheepdog at work herding sheep (see my painting on page 63), horses grazing in a field (this page), a puppy playing for the first time in snow, or a cat lying asleep in its favourite sunny spot in the garden. The choices are infinite, but a certain amount of critical observation, assisted perhaps by photographs, will bring your outdoor scenes to life.

Start with the horizon or skyline. A low horizon showing

your chosen animal tall against a plain sky gives the picture impact and immediately elevates the animal to a position of importance. For example, the watercolour painting of the steeplechaser, *High Clouds*, on pages 52-53 has a low horizon as the horse is of paramount importance in this picture.

Consider also the effects of light and the weather. You should know what sort of day you are trying to depict. Sunshine will cause strong shadows to appear in a painting if it is a bright summer's day. Shadows are longer when cast by an early-morning or late-afternoon sun, while at midday they are very short. They are softer and less noticeable if the day is overcast when there may be a more even, overall light. Colours are affected by these conditions, too. Grass may seem greener on a bright summer's day, duller and greyer on an autumn afternoon. All such details are important when painting an outdoor scene and you should always make notes about these things in your sketchbook so that you can incorporate them into your painting later.

Distance, too, alters the way we see things. There is less contrast the nearer one gets to the horizon; small details become invisible and differences are neutralized. Hills on the horizon merge into the colour of the sky against which they sit. So, on a bright day they would be bluer than on a dull day when they might look grey. In a bright evening sunset they might take on the reds and purples of the sky to the extent that they lose their own colour identity. The opposite is true as you move closer – details stand out more and everything retains its original colour.

Interior Backgrounds
An interior view will be used to show an animal's home or natural environment. It may be horses in a stable, as in my painting here of the mare and foal in their loose-box, or a dog in your living-room on his favourite armchair (which is probably yours, too!). A mischievous Siamese kitten may be better shown playing with a ball of wool than just sitting still on the floor.

It is important when painting backgrounds to take into consideration the light source. Is there a source of light creating contrasts between light and dark? In a stable we may see a single beam of light acting as a spotlight and catching a horse's face in great detail, but softening the background into subtle shades of colour where other objects, such as riding tackle, are only guessed at. This would be achieved by restricting everything to a very close range of dark colours and tones, perhaps six or seven similar mixtures, derived mainly from Burnt Umber, Burnt Sienna and Black.

Abstract Backgrounds
On the other hand, you may wish to omit all subject matter from the background and just use the colours of the animal to enhance its portrait in an abstract fashion. You can dab or stipple similar colours to those used on the body (as in

the painting of the Alsatian in oils on pages 30-33) to achieve a more abstract background. This stops the background being flat and boring but does not detract from the main subject. It is a good idea to place lighter colours in the background against darker ones on the animal and vice versa. The lower part of the painting should always be slightly darker than the upper to give weight to the whole painting (see the watercolour painting of Dinky the cat, on page 37).

Background Details
Just how much detail you include in a background is, of course, up to you. You must decide whether you are going to draw every leaf on a tree or just depict the larger patterns of light and dark. The problem can often be resolved by a clear understanding of your main aims and intentions. If you are predominantly interested in the animal's portrait you should limit your background detail to a minimum. If, however, it is a scene or pattern which contains an animal as part of the whole picture, rather than as its major feature, you should draw and paint detail throughout the foreground and middle distance.

It is in your choice of background that you make decisions that affect the overall look of your painting. Elsewhere, observation and accuracy are your watchwords, but here pictorial awareness is also called for. With practice, however, it is not difficult to make these decisions because you subconsciously become aware of which type of background suits your needs best. In reading this you have probably already dismissed some of the choices as not for you. On the other hand, an alternative may have been put forward which will seem attractive and which could give your picture added zest.

PAINTING BACKGROUNDS
THE STEEPLECHASER 'HIGH CLOUDS'
IN WATERCOLOUR

Fig. 34

Fig. 35

For this example of a painting with an outdoor background which I will take you through, I chose a fairly heavy rough surface Saunders watercolour paper (285gm²). It is expensive but well worth it for the extra control you have when using washes of colour. This paper is heavy enough not to need damping and stretching and does not cockle even after generous applications of water. It can be pinned straight on to your board. You can work the wet into wet method or dryer brush techniques equally well on this paper. It also takes light pencil work effectively and gentle rubbing out does not damage it.

The colours I used in my palette were: Ivory Black, Viridian, Cobalt Blue, Yellow Ochre, Cadmium Yellow, Lemon Yellow, Burnt Umber and Crimson Alizarin. No White was needed as I let the paper show through. I used only a Series 40 Sable No. 8 brush. The tip of the brush I used for very fine work and the full brush for broad sweeps and for thicker areas of colour.

First, decide on the height of your horizon. The horse should dominate and a low horizon emphasizes this. You will notice that throughout this painting I have moved from one area to another rather than finishing one section completely before going on to the next. There are two reasons for this – one is to allow certain areas to dry out so that a colour will not run into the adjacent one and the other reason is that it helps to keep the colours throughout the picture in harmony so that you can see how one will look against another as you paint.

Indicate the horizon lightly with an HB pencil and then carefully draw the outline of the horse using as few lines as

possible (see fig. 34). Remember, once a pencil line is washed over with colour it cannot be removed, so you do not want unnecessary ones to show. Next draw in the landscape behind the horse with your pencil. Having done the preliminary drawing stand back and look at it. Now is the time to lift off any unwanted pencil lines with a putty rubber. It will be too late once you have started painting over the outline.

For the sky make a pale mix of Cobalt Blue using plenty of water and wash it across the top of the picture from left to right taking it carefully around and under the horse and overlapping into the trees, so that, when they are painted in, tiny gaps of sky will show through the foliage (see fig. 35). While the sky is still damp, run a stronger mix of blue into the upper section of the picture leaving areas of the paler tone to give the impression of clouds. With this same mixture, add the blue to the distant hills which show low down by the right-hand group of trees. Now start to paint the horse. Make a pale mix of Cadmium Yellow and a little Burnt Umber and using plenty of water and the tip of the brush, paint the ears and then, with a fully-loaded brush, sweep the colour over the whole body except the white blaze on his forehead and his mane and tail.

One point to notice: the hooves are hidden in the grass. If you were to paint them in it would immediately make the grass look like a flat carpet rather than growing grass. Obviously, if the horse was standing in a stable yard or on the road you would paint the hooves but not in this case. Now paint the group of tall trees on the left. For this you will need a mixture of Viridian with a touch of Cobalt Blue

Fig. 36 The steeplechaser *High Clouds* 41 × 51cm (16 × 20in)

and a tiny dip of Black mixed generously together using plenty of water. With dabbing strokes start at the top of the trees and fill in the big group, not forgetting to leave bits of sky showing through in places. Run the wash across and down to the base of the tree group. Repeat this with the clump of trees on the right of the picture. Then, with a paler shade of the same mixture, wash in the distant hills gradually fading them out where they lead across the horizon to the right. With the same pale tone, paint right across the centre of the field leaving areas of white showing in places. Now, rinse the brush and using Lemon Yellow and a touch of Cadmium Yellow flow a pale wash over the highlighted trees in the middle distance, working across the picture and also in the foreground as shown in **fig. 35**. With a little more Cadmium Yellow, fill in the yellow area where a mass of buttercups catch the light under the distant trees. Now return to the horse (see **fig. 36**). With Burnt Umber and a little Black, paint in his mane and tail. Leave the original pale wash as highlights on the horse. Generously mix Yellow Ochre, a touch of Burnt Umber and Crimson Alizarin for darker mid-tones on his head, neck and body. Enrich with more Crimson Alizarin for the broad pattern of strong darks on the legs and under the belly. Then mix Burnt Umber, Crimson Alizarin and Black and, using the point of the brush, draw in the nostril, mouth and eye, leaving the highlight on the eye pupil clear. Finally, add more Black for the darkest tones on the mane and tail.

Enrich the mixture with an addition of Burnt Umber and a little more Crimson Alizarin and run in the broad patterns of darker tones on the head, neck, the top of the shoulders, along the back and over the top of the rib cage, and the hindquarters. Then turn to the legs, darkening the distant fore and hind legs where they are in shadow. Strengthen the tone under the belly and again, where there is deep shadow at the top of the shoulder, the base of the neck, on the chest, and behind the forelegs where the belly starts.

Now to the final painting of the landscape. Make a wash of pure Lemon Yellow and paint the lightest tones of the trees in the middle distance right across the picture. Run some of this colour into the foreground and into the distant patch of buttercups. Add a little Cadmium Yellow to your mix, and then take this wash again over the lighter trees and the hills in the middle distance. This will add warmth to the painting. Now make a mix of Viridian with a little Black added and boldly paint the deep shadows in the foliage of the left-hand group of trees. Also wash this colour along under the hedgerows. Use a paler tone of this to indicate the clumps of foliage and with the tip of your brush paint the tree trunks in the right-hand group of trees. For the grass you should try to give the effect of clumps and tussocks – grass is never even and all one colour. Make a rich mix of Cadmium Yellow with Cobalt Blue, use plenty of water and paint the grass with short, sharp, brush strokes. Work in this way over and across the field from left to right. Shorten your brush strokes even more as you paint the foreground. Don't be afraid to allow white to show through here and there in the grass. It will add sparkle and brilliance. To finish, add a little more Black to the mix to make a very dark tone and paint the shadow cast by the horse.

53

EXERCISE FIVE
SIAMESE CATS
IN PASTEL

Fig. 37

Ideally, cats must be in a relaxed mood if you are to paint them well, so it is better to draw them in their own home and then paint them back at your studio. For this picture I did a number of quick sketches of the cats in different poses before making accurate drawings. As I was to paint the cats together, I had to decide upon the best composition. My final choice of positioning was to show two different poses with one animal almost in profile and the other in a three-quarter view (**fig. 37**). This is another exercise I will take you through step-by-step.

I chose a tinted paper (sand-coloured, medium-grained Fabriano Ingres as it provided a ready-made background on which the animals really stood out. These cats have lovely creamy colouring with dark points on their ears, masks, legs and tails. Their beautiful blue-green eyes show in fine contrast to the sand-coloured background.

Firstly, pad your drawing board with several thicknesses of newspaper, or any old scrap paper, so that if there are any uneven places on the board they will not make a bump in the Ingres paper. Also, it makes a more pleasant surface on which to work. Next, pin the Ingres paper over this on to the board with drawing pins, smoothing it as tight as possible with your hand. Do remember to wash your hands

before touching the paper as any grease from them will mark it.

I find it a great help to use an old mount, preferably in dark cardboard the size of the proposed picture, to frame the area on your paper where the cats are to be drawn (see page 15). In this case the mount would have to measure 25 × 41cm (10 × 16in). Place this 'frame' on your paper so that your eye will adjust to this size when drawing the initial outline. There is nothing more infuriating than sketching out your drawing and then finding it is too large or too small for the selected picture size.

Take a 4B pencil and lightly draw the outline of the cats, using very little pressure or you will dent the paper. When you feel your drawing is correct, lift off any surplus lines with a putty rubber to keep it as simple and clear as possible (**fig. 38**). It is much easier to erase errors at this stage!

With a penknife rather than a pencil sharpener (which will usually break the point) sharpen a medium black charcoal pencil and very carefully draw over the outline of the cats (**fig. 39**). Then shade in, with faint lines close together, the patterns made by the dark markings on the cats. Now fill in these lightly shaded areas with pastel

54

Fig. 38

Fig. 39

Burnt Umber Tint 4. You should then darken the ears, masks, legs and tails even more by working black charcoal pencil into the Burnt Umber Tint 4. For the cream body colouring on both animals use the side of a broken stick of pastel Yellow Ochre Tint 0. I often break a pastel in half and use the side rather than the tip for wide areas of colour as it gives a broader sweep of colour, ideal for emphasizing the contours of the body.

Now look at the eyes of both cats. They are made up of several colours. Paint tiny strokes of Coeruleum Tint 0, then Prussian Blue Tint 3 and, finally, tiny dots of Sap Green Tint 1 to add sparkle. The pupils are half-dilated and shown as a V-shape which you should draw in black charcoal pencil. The centre top of the V makes the highlight (see **fig. 39**).

You should now start to consolidate the work that you have already done. In this stage, (**fig. 40**), you want to give weight to the bodies, delineate the bone structure of both animals and their muscles and finally add the texture of the overlying fur. The dark markings on the heads outline the underlying shape of the skull where the smooth fur is stretched over the cheek-bones, nose and bones around the eyes. The different weight and strength with which you apply pastel can give the impression of different textures.

With Yellow Ochre Tint 0 and using short strokes to indicate fur, work over the light area of the reclining cat gradually building it up until it looks solid. Add a highlight on the shoulder, upper arm, forehead and stomach with White pastel. Then, with Burnt Umber Tint 4, blend along the back and into the cream of the body. You also need to consolidate the pale brown markings on the legs, tail, head and ears. For the mid-dark tones use Burnt Umber Tint 6 and for the deepest colour work in Black pastel. To give the effect of longer hairs over shorter, draw them in with tiny strokes of contrasting dark and light colours. The paw pads are drawn with black charcoal pencil and the highlights on the soft pads with Cool Grey Tint 4. Work the pink inside the cat's ears with Autumn Brown Tint 3 and tone into the dark interior with strokes of black charcoal pencil. Leave the final touches to the eyes until the next stage.

Now turn to the sitting cat. It is richer and darker in colour throughout than the reclining cat. To mould the face use strokes of black charcoal pencil enriched by the addition of Burnt Sienna Tint 8 on the forehead, muzzle and above the eye. This colour is also added to the black on the far ear. The front of the legs, paws and the hind legs are worked in black charcoal pencil, as is the tail and the line of the back. Now work Burnt Sienna Tint 8 into the back with strokes following the direction of the fur. Do the tail in the same way working along its length from root to tip. Then place highlights of Purple Grey Tint 2 on the legs, the paws and tail, and similarly on the forehead, nose and cheek-bones. Work the shape of the body with light, flowing strokes of Yellow Ochre Tint 0. Next, with Burnt Umber Tint 4, indicate the direction of the fur over the body and chest, particularly emphasizing the way the hair changes direction over the hindquarters, rib cage and stomach. Strengthen the colour where the fur folds in under the stomach with a few flowing lines of Burnt Sienna Tint 8, and draw some individual groups of hair on the chest and between the front legs using the black charcoal pencil.

For the pink inside of the ears use Autumn Brown Tint 3, and black charcoal pencil for the darker interior, indicating the moulding of the ear and the short hairs inside with the same pencil and a touch of Cool Grey Tint 2.

If you look at my final painting (**fig. 41**) you may think that there is not much difference between it and **fig. 40**. But if you look again there are certain changes. I decided that the nose of the sitting cat was too long, so I shortened the end of it and filled in more dark on the bridge of the nose. I also slightly exaggerated the moulding of the muzzle and made the upper lip more rounded, thus softening the cat's facial expression. The whiskers were also added at this stage; just touched in with very faint lines of a sharpened black charcoal pencil – you don't want them to look like steel wire!

I also decided to add some more detail to the reclining cat and, using the black charcoal pencil, I faintly drew in some long hairs where the hind leg joins the stomach, and indicated where the fur parts slightly between the neck and the shoulder. I felt that the sitting cat's body should look more solid and dark so I strengthened the dark areas.

The eyes of both cats needed a bit more colour so I added a firmer touch of Sap Green Tint 1, with the deep blue on the inner and outer corners strengthened with more Prussian Blue Tint 3. The upper section of the V-shaped pupils should be left clear, with the paper showing through as a highlight. The eyes of Siamese cats are beautiful and so I wanted to make sure that they really sparkled in my painting.

There are many little details and finishing touches to add to a painting that may seem finished at first glance. But don't be tempted to overdo the detail; it is sometimes better to leave a painting simple rather than add too many fussy touches to it. However, with practice you will know when to add details and when to stop. It's all a matter of observation.

Fig. 40

Fig. 41

EXERCISE SIX
MY DOG
IN OILS

Fig. 42

Fig. 43

One of the first reactions of the owner of a loved animal is to wish to have its likeness to keep for always. It is good to have photographs but to be able to make a drawing or painting is much more satisfactory. But how do we go about it?

It is really essential to make careful drawings of the animal in different positions because for a good portrait the pose must look as natural as possible. Look carefully at the different drawings of Dodie, my tricoloured Beagle (figs. 42, 43, 44 and 46). I wanted to paint her in oils but couldn't make up my mind on the best pose. Eventually however, I decided to use the pose where she is sitting up watching my every movement (figs. 44 and 47).

For my drawings, I used a large sketchbook, 4B and 6B pencils and a black ballpoint pen. I also used coloured Conté to lend a little touch of colour and give the drawings

a feeling of solidity and tone. It is useful to take down lots of notes about eyes, nose, muzzle, position of ears, details of legs and paws etc. as these will prove invaluable when you attempt the full portrait.

For my painting, I used a canvas board, size 51 × 41cm (20 × 16in), positioned on my easel lengthwise to best suit the dimensions of the pose. I left the canvas board white to lend brilliance to the painting and using a Series 220 Nylon No. 2 filbert-shaped brush and turpentine only for medium, I sketched in the pose. Be careful to position the animal correctly on the canvas allowing room at the top and bottom so the painting doesn't look cramped.

It is a good idea to start with a few guidelines to help you get the size and proportions right. For instance, Dodie's head is a blunt-ended triangle with the ears angled on either side. I dropped a line down the centre of the

Fig. 44

forehead to the nose and another from the middle of each ear to help me position the shoulders and forelegs. This line from the forehead also dropped down the nose and continued through the centre of Dodie's chest and acted as a guide to the placing of the hind leg and paw. The barrel shape of her tummy swung to the right with the powerful, muscled foreleg cutting across it. Her front paws turned slightly outwards. The foreshortened (see pages 16-17) right hind leg was angled in towards the viewer with the paw in three-quarter view coming in behind the right forepaw. The curve of her back swung down along the barrel shape and through the haunch and foreshortened hind leg and finished in the sweep of the tail.

It is important to note the comparative sizes of parts of an animal's body and the finer individual details that give the animal its character. For example, Dodie is fairly broad between the eyes: in fact almost the width of one of her pricked ears. There are slight wrinkles on her forehead and darker markings which extend down to her shiny black nose. The nose, viewed from the front, is heart-shaped and extra care is needed to portray this correctly. Her upper lip under the nose is gently curved and her muzzle very soft but well defined with prominent whisker follicles (see details in **fig. 45**).

Exactness in the initial drawing is all important because if the proportions are not correct at this stage the whole painting will be wrong, endless corrections will be necessary and as a result the spontaneity of the picture will be lost.

Step back and compare your work with your subject at every opportunity to check that you are progressing well.

The limited palette of colours I used throughout this

Fig. 45

Fig. 47

form – building slowly by degrees and not finishing one part before another.

Never work for too long at one time and take frequent breaks. When you return to your painting with a fresh eye you may be able to see alterations which are needed.

After I had filled in the main drawing and dark tones I started to work on the details. Dodie's white areas were painted with Titanium White, toned down with a touch of Yellow Ochre for the creamier parts and a little Black added for grey shadows. For the brown areas I used Yellow Ochre, with Cadmium Yellow added for the richer colour, and a touch of Crimson Alizarin for the deepest browns. The highlights on the forehead, ears, face and nose were pale grey, made by mixing White and a little Black. Dodie's darkest markings on her back and tail were done with Burnt Umber and Black.

The subtle details that make your animal an individual should be carefully noted. For instance, Dodie has certain characteristics which make her different – the way she sits, how she holds her head and ears and particularly her expressive eyes. The hair follicles above the eyes, corresponding to human eyebrows, hold particular expression in a dog, as does the set of its ears. Dodie's ears are soft and silky and her coat is thick with a sheen. These details need to be shown. Be careful always to follow the direction of hair growth with your brush strokes and note where the light falls so that you can pick out the highlights and tones of a coat. See pages 36–37 for more details on painting hair and fur.

I used cool grey (a mixture of White with a touch of Black) to highlight the pupil of the eye as this avoids the harshness of using plain White which can often give an animal a staring expression (see fig. 45 for detail). Then I carefully painted the details of the black nose with grey highlights, grey muzzle, creamy paws and cream and black toe-nails to finish off the painting.

Finally, I studied my painting and checked every detail. All I needed to complete the painting was a suitable frame to complement Dodie's portrait.

painting were: Titanium White, Ivory Black, Cadmium Yellow, Yellow Ochre, Burnt Umber and Crimson Alizarin.

Having drawn the dog's outline on the board I took a Series 120 Nylon No. 4 brush and using Burnt Umber and turpentine as a medium I blocked in the main masses and shapes. I then started to put in the darkest darks and masses, using Series 220 Nylon flat, square-ended Nos. 5 and 8 brushes. I used a combination of Dodie's coat colours to paint a background of broken colour – Yellow Ochre, Cadmium Yellow, Burnt Umber mixed with a little White and Black – putting on the colour with short brush strokes. I was careful to place the dark background areas behind the lighter parts of Dodie and vice versa, thus managing to avoid a hard line but still making her stand out (see fig. 47).

After this initial work I went on to use equal parts of turpentine and linseed oil as medium and progressed with the picture working it all up together – background against

Fig. 46

M Parric Williams.

EXERCISE SEVEN
SHEEPDOG AND SHEEP
IN PASTEL

Fig. 48

Fig. 49

I have often watched sheepdog trials and been fascinated and enthralled to see those patient sheepdogs rounding up and driving reluctant sheep into a small pen. It is a true battle of wills between the dog and the sheep. In this pastel painting I have tried to capture some of the atmosphere of the sheep stamping in anger, the dog creeping closer and

closer until, at the last moment, the sheep turn and bol into the pen. For sketching scenes like this, either from th television or in the countryside, I generally use a blac ballpoint pen and a Rowney spiral-bound sketchboo (PBSI). The pen flows easily over the smooth paper and i is an ideal medium for rapid sketching. I made a numbe

sketch notes of the sheep in many different positions
d then made a rough composition of the picture to make
e that I had got everything in proportion.

On to a fawn-tinted Ingres pastel paper and using a 4B
ncil, I copied very lightly the composition I had decided
from my sketchbook. I worked on the smooth side of
e paper so that the lines would be easier to control (fig.
. Any corrections should be made at this stage with a
tty rubber.

With a sharpened medium black charcoal pencil, I care-
ly drew over the 4B pencil lines of the original drawing
d lightly hatched in the dark areas on the animals. Then
ng a white Conté I filled in all the pale areas on the
mals. I put no detail in at this stage (fig. 49).

It is at the final stage (fig. 50) that the picture is pulled
ether and strengthened. The sheep in the pen in the
ckground are not painted in detail as the focal point in
painting is made by the sheepdog and the recalcitrant
ep in the foreground. The sheep-pen was given more
inition by adding Burnt Umber Tint 4 on the shaded
as of the bars and then darkening them with black
rcoal pencil. Next, I added a little more detail to the
wing of the group of sheep using the black charcoal
ncil and working on their heads, ears, eyes and legs. For
bulky bodies covered with fleece I used Vandyke
own Tint 2 and for the darker mid-tones, Madder
own Tint 0. I used Yellow Ochre Tint 0 for the
hlights.

I then turned my concentration to the single sheep in
foreground and drew it in detail with the black charcoal
ncil. First I worked the ears and head, taking care to
w the skull formation beneath the smooth dark hair on

the head. Note the U-shape of the nose and beneath it the
central line above the upper lips where they curve away on
either side. Notice also the way that the ears lie at an angle
of almost 45 degrees to the head. A horse's ears, for example, are more upright in comparison. I emphasized the
curls of fleece with black charcoal pencil for the darkest
areas, Vandyke Brown Tint 2 for the rich tones, Yellow
Ochre Tint 0 for the creamy colouring, and Madder Brown
Tint 0 and White (Cream shade) for the highlights. Other
anatomical features to note are that sheep seem to have
very thin legs compared to the weight of their fleecy bodies,
but when they are shorn they seem more in proportion.
They also tend to be knock-kneed but make up for this by
having very neat little hooves! It is useful to make these
kinds of observations in your sketchbook before you start
drawing or painting, especially if it is an animal you have
not painted before.

I drew the dog in detail with the black charcoal pencil.
I filled in the dark areas of his coat with the side of a black
Conté but left the paper showing through in places for the
lighter tones. The sheen on the coat was laid in with Cool
Grey Tint 4 pastel and the white markings were painted in
with white Conté with a touch of Yellow Ochre Tint 0
pastel for added lightness in places. The dog's long curly
fur and his heavy ruff around the neck were carefully
drawn with a black charcoal pencil while his brown eye
was filled in with Burnt Umber Tint 4 and the highlight
with a touch of white Conté. I wanted to leave the grass
impressionistic so this was just very lightly shaded in with
pale Sap Green Tint 5 and the darker tones with Sap
Green Tint 8 and black charcoal pencil. And there you
have the finished painting – full of life and movement.

ACKNOWLEDGEMENTS

My special thanks for their unfailing help and patience in the making of this book are due to: Royston Davies; Joan Clibbon, Robin Wood and Cathy Gosling at Collins; David Rose, Peter Garrard, and John Youé and his team. Also, thanks to Michael Petts for the main body of the photographs, Tony Latham for the photograph on page 51 and for Figs. 16, 20, 21, 23 & 24 and Chromogene for the photograph of the polo ponies on page 46.

My sincere thanks also go to the following owners w kindly gave permission for the reproduction of the portra and drawings of their animals: Mr & Mrs Austen, Mr Mrs Blackman, Dr Evelyn Churches, Mrs Burton and M Scouler, Mrs Clifford-Turner, the Goulbourne fami Miss Jennifer Hardy, Mr & Mrs Hope, Mr & Mrs Walla Maddocks, Mr & Mrs Vickers, Mr & Mrs Chapman a Mr & Mrs Christopherson. Thanks also to *Leisure Pain* magazine for permission to reproduce the pictures on pag 14-17 and 58-61.

And I am particularly grateful to my family and frien both two- and four-legged, whose encouragement and c operation made this book possible.